AAT

DIPLOMA PATHWAY

LEVEL 3 DIPLOMA FOR ACCOUNTING
TECHNICIANS (QCF)

COMBINED **COMPANION** Unit 32

Professional Ethics

BPP
LEARNING MEDIA

Third edition June 2009
First edition 2005

ISBN 9780 7517 6712 4 (previous edition 0 7517 3212 2)

British Library Cataloguing-in-Publication Data
A catalogue record for this book is available from the British Library

Published by

BPP Learning Media Ltd,
BPP House,
Aldine Place,
London, W12 8AA

Printed in the United Kingdom

CONTENTS

Introduction   (v)
The structure of the standards for Unit 32   (vi)
Note on the AAT Guidelines on Professional Ethics   (xi)

Course Companion

1   Ethical decision-making   3

2   Identifying ethical issues   23

3   Personal and interpersonal skills   47

4   Ethics for members in business   65

5   Ethics for members in practice   87

Answers to chapter activities   119

How much have you learned? – answers   127

Revision Companion

	Questions	Answers
Chapter activities		
1 Ethical decision-making	139	159
2 Identifying ethical issues	141	161
3 Personal and interpersonal skills	143	163
4 Ethics for members in businesss	145	165
5 Ethics for members in practice	147	167
AAT specimen simulation	149	169
Index		179

INTRODUCTION

BPP Learning Media's Companions range of AAT materials offers lecturers and students a compact alternative to its traditional range, and is ideal for students who like to grips with the essentials and study on the move.

The range comprises:

- **Course Companions**, covering all the Knowledge & Understanding and Performance Criteria specified by the Standards of Competence and needed by students, with numerous illustrations, practical examples and activities for students to use to consolidate their learning.

- **Revision Companions**, ideal for classroom courses, which contain an additional range of graded activities for each chapter of the Course Companion, plus specially written practice assessment and answers for the Unit, and the AAT's own specimen assessment. Full answers to all activities and assessments, prepared by BPP Learning Media, are included.

- **Tutor Companions**, providing a further bank of questions, answers and practice assessment for classroom use, available separately only to lecturers whose colleges adopt the Companions for the relevant Unit.

This is the third edition of BPP's Combined Companion for AAT Unit 32 (Diploma pathway) *Professional Ethics*. It has been stringently reviewed by subject experts and has been carefully designed to enable students to practise all aspects of the requirements of the Standards of Competence and performance criteria, and ultimately be successful in their assessments.

The Course Companion section (Chapters 1–5) contains:

- Clear, step by step explanation of the topic

- Logical progression and linking from one chapter to the next, using a case study approach throughout

- Numerous illustrations and practical examples

- Interactive activities within the text, with answers supplied

The Revision Companion section contains:

- Graded activities corresponding to each chapter of the Course Companion, with answers

- A skills based assessment (the AAT's own specimen assessment) with full answers prepared by BPP Learning Media.

Tutors adopting our Companions (minimum of ten Course Companions and ten Revision Companions per Unit, or ten Combined Companions as appropriate) are entitled to free access to the Lecturers' Area resources, including the Tutor Companion. To obtain your log-in, e-mail lecturersvc@bpp.com.

Home Study students are also entitled to access to additional resources. You will have received your log-in details on registration.

If you have any comments about this book, please e-mail helendarch@bpp.com or write to Helen Darch, AAT Publishing Manager, BPP Learning Media Ltd, BPP House, Aldine Place, London W12 8AA.

THE STRUCTURE OF THE STANDARDS FOR UNIT 32

The Unit is divided into **elements of competence** describing activities which the individual should be able to perform.

Each element includes:

a)   A set of performance criteria. This defines what constitutes competence performance.

b)   A range statement. This defines the situations, contexts, methods etc in which competence should be displayed.

In addition, there is a statement of the **knowledge and understanding** which underpin competence in the Unit's elements.

The elements of competence for Unit 32 are set out below. Knowledge and understanding required for the unit as a whole are listed first, followed by the performance criteria and range statements for each element. Performance criteria are cross-referenced below to chapters in this Companion.

Unit 32 Standards of competence

Unit commentary

There is no specific assessed unit relating exclusively to ethics within the AAT Accounting Qualification NVQ/SVQ pathway. The AAT has, however, provided guidance to its members clearly identifying expected and acceptable behaviour in relation to ethics. As the unit is new there are few comparisons to be drawn or indicative mapping to be made against current units.

The Professional Ethics unit requires the candidate to provide evidence of their ability to demonstrate the ethical duties and responsibilities necessary and the knowledge required to underpin ethical practice in this section.

The unit has been developed using the existing AAT Guidelines on Professional Ethics (based upon principles approved by the International Federation of Accountants, IFAC). From this basis, the key components have been extracted and assimilated to reflect the most critical requirements for professional conduct and competence in this field.

The Professional Ethics unit is not designed to replicate the ethical requirements detailed by the professional sponsoring bodies of the AAT. However, it provides a sound basis for progression in application of ethics and related knowledge and understanding required of students at the higher level.

In addition to the specific learning outcomes for this unit, the ethics subject matter forms an ideal basis for developing the candidate's communication skills, at a level sufficient to provide a smoother progression for candidates from level 3 to level 4. The AAT National Archive Forum identified recently that candidates' communication skills were an area that could benefit from further enhancement to provide a smoother transition to level 4. This unit also provides an ideal forum to develop critical decision making skills.

The unit can be taken at either level 3 or level 4.

Elements contained within this unit are:

Element 32.1   Apply general principles and procedures for ethical compliance expected within the accounting sector

Element 32.2   Develop, maintain and apply ethics in employer/employee situations

Element 32.3   Develop, maintain and apply ethics in public practice

Knowledge and understanding

To perform this unit effectively you will need to know and understand:

1   The guidelines of your professional body, including professional liability and negligence

2   A principle-based approach to professional ethics

3   Legal considerations (UK or own country), with particular consideration of:

   –   The common types of fraud (see also Element 10.2)
   –   Ownership of records
   –   Lien: retention of books and other documentation

Element 32.1 Apply general principles and procedures for ethical compliance expected within the accounting sector

Performance criteria
   Chapter(s)

In order to perform this element successfully you need to:

A   Identify and apply the *fundamental principles* of honesty and integrity   1

B   Highlight *situations within professional work* that require objectivity and fairness, and where judgements and actions could compromise personal or *organisational* integrity and reputation   1, 2

C   Recognise the principles of effective *Continuing Professional Development* (CPD) to maintain professional and technical competence (to include sources of advice and information outside formal learning).   3

D   Recognise and explain why certain types of information should be regarded as confidential   2

E   Identify circumstances when it would be appropriate to *disclose confidential information*   2

F   Identify the key issues which ensure *professional services* are performed within the scope of professional ethics guidance   2, 4, 5

G   Make critical decisions to identify appropriate ethical behaviour when interacting with others in a variety of circumstances   1

H   Refer and seek advice from relevant sources for issues beyond own   1, 3
     professional competence

Chapter(s)

I   Describe the types of *contractual* obligations you would have in providing   2, 5
     services to clients, to include due care and carrying out assignments within
     a reasonable timescale

J   Discuss, agree and resolve any ethical conflict   1, 3

Range statement

Performance in this element relates to the following contexts:

- *Fundamental principles:*

    –   Integrity
    –   Objectivity
    –   Professional and technical competence
    –   Due care
    –   Confidentiality
    –   Professional behaviour

- *Professional work situations:*

    –   Provision of services as self-employed
    –   Preparation of financial statements for client or own organisation
    –   Performance of internal audit services
    –   Provision of financial management services
    –   Acceptance of gifts

- *Organisational:*

    –   HM Revenue & Customs
    –   Client organisations
    –   Employer
    –   Professional bodies

- *Sources of information for CPD:*

    –   The Internet
    –   Professional journals
    –   Professional body network opportunities
    –   Organisational/company training updates

- *Confidential information/disclosure:*

    –   Basic duties
    –   Usage
    –   Non disclosure and disclosure (when expressly authorised by client, or legal, regulatory
         or professional body)

- *Professional services:*

    –   Taxation
    –   VAT calculations
    –   Financial management consultancy

- *Contractual:*

  Nature of service/contract (to include performance and responsibilities by whom, for whom, by when, fees, due care, ownership and lien)

- *Communication and personal skills:*

  Communication with peers, superiors, clients, external bodies and agencies, and including specifically skills of negotiation, critical decision-making, discussion, letter and report writing

Element 32.2 Develop, maintain and apply ethics in employer/employee situations

Performance criteria
Chapter(s)

In order to perform this element successfully you need to:

A	Describe the type of *culture* within organisations which supports and promotes high ethical values and helps resolve any conflict of loyalties	4
B	Resolve conflicting loyalties where an employer may ask you to perform tasks which are illegal, unethical or against the rules of standards of the accounting profession	4
C	Follow appropriate *procedures* where you believe an employer has committed or will commit an *act which you believe to be illegal or unethical*	4
D	Respond appropriately to requests to work outside the confines of your own professional experience and expertise	4

Range statement

Performance in this element relates to the following contexts:

- *Cultural values:*

  - Openness
  - Trust
  - Integrity
  - Respect
  - Empowerment
  - Accountability

- *Procedures:*

  - Seek confidential independent or professional counselling and advice
  - Keep accurate records of meetings/discussions
  - Persuade employer not to perpetrate action
  - Advise client of ethical and legal considerations
  - 'Enforced' resignation

- *Acts (illegal or unethical):*

  - Fraud
  - Other illegal activity
  - Falsification of records
  - Supply of information or statements which are misleading, false or deceptive
  - Client influence

- Employer influence
- Actions of delegated staff

Performance in this element relates to professional conduct with: peers, employers, superiors and subordinates.

Element 32.3 Develop, maintain and apply ethics in public practice

Performance criteria
Chapter(s)

In order to perform this element successfully you need to:

A   Prepare appropriate letters of engagement and develop and implement a fair fees policy for your professional services   5

B   Identify and explain how *specific situations can undermine professional independence.*   5

C   Prepare a policy to be followed for handling clients' monies   5

D   Maintain independence and objectivity and impartiality in a range of circumstances   5

E   Make *recommendations for a policy statement* in relation to a client wishing to change accountant   5

F   Identify scope of professional liability   5

G   Prepare clear guidelines which should be followed to advertise your accounting services in a professional and ethical manner   5

H   Give advice to clients on retention of books, working papers and other documents   5

Range statement

Performance in this element relates to the following contexts:

- *Specific situations and professional independence:*

  - Simultaneous engagement in other related business
  - Ownership or interest in client's companies
  - Personal and family relationships
  - Agency commission

- *Recommendations on policy on performing recurring work for a client:*

  - which has been or is currently being undertaken by another professional advisor

  - in relation to instructions by another advisor who is taking over work that you are currently performing for a client

Performance in this element can relate to the following contexts of Self Employment: Accounting Services Work assignments such as taxation, reporting, accounting services and advertising of such services.

NOTE ON THE AAT GUIDELINES ON PROFESSIONAL ETHICS

The standards for Unit 32 were originally based on the AAT Guidelines on Professional Ethics which came into effect in January 2000. These guidelines:

- Took a **principle-based approach** to professional ethics, based on fundamental general ethical principles (integrity, objectivity, professional and technical competence, due care, confidentiality and professional behaviour)

- Gave specific **guidance on the application in practice** of the fundamental principles in a number of typical situations occuring in the accountancy profession.

A new set of (far more substantial) Guidelines on Professional Ethics was introduced in May 2008. These guidelines are quite differently organised, structured around:

- A **conceptual framework** or methodology for handling ethical issues, consisting of:

    - The fundamental **principles** (as in the earlier guidelines)

    - Identification and evaluation of **threats** to the fundamental principles

    - Implementing **safeguards** to eliminate or reduce threats to an acceptable level, so that compliance with the fundamental principles is not compromised

    - **Declining or discontinuing** the professional activity involved, if appropriate safeguards cannot be implemented.

- Guidance on **how the conceptual framework can be applied in practice** (with examples of threats and safeguards in each area)

- Extensive **examples of application** of the framework in a range of specific situations (many of which will be beyond the scope of the Unit 32 standards)

It is not yet clear to what extent the authors of Unit 32 assessments will rely on the structure and content of the 2008 guidelines, where these are different in approach and scope to the performance criteria set out in the standards.

This Course Companion remains faithful to the structure, approach and content of the standards. However, in this edition, we have:

- Added coverage of the **conceptual framework**

- Added '**Threats and safeguards**' checklists, to suggest how the conceptual framework can be applied

- Used the revised **terminology** of the new guidelines.

    - 'Employed members' (2000) has now become 'Members in business' (2008)
    - 'Self-employed members' (2000) has now become 'Members in practice' (2008)

- Added '**Signposts**', directing you to relevant sections of the 2008 Guidelines. We strongly recommend that you obtain a copy of the Guidelines (which can be downloaded from the AAT website), for use as a supplement to this workbook.

COURSE COMPANION UNIT 32

chapter 1:
ETHICAL DECISION-MAKING

chapter coverage 📖

In this initial chapter, we consider the fundamental principles of ethical conduct, as they apply to the general accounting context.

We also consider, in general terms, how ethical dilemmas and conflicts can arise – and how they can be resolved, using the conceptual framework set out in the AAT's Guidelines on Professional Ethics. (In chapter 2, we look more specifically at situations in professional work where ethical issues may arise, together with guidelines on how to deal with them.)

The topics we shall cover are:

✍ What are ethics?

✍ Why behave ethically?

✍ Ethical principles

✍ Identifying appropriate ethical behaviours

✍ The concepual framework

✍ Dealing with ethical conflicts

KNOWLEDGE AND UNDERSTANDING AND PERFORMANCE CRITERIA COVERAGE

Knowledge and understanding

- The guidelines of your professional body
- A principle-based approach to professional ethics
- Legal considerations

Performance criteria – Element 32.1

- Identify and apply the fundamental principles of honesty and integrity
- Highlight situations within professional work that require objectivity and fairness, and where judgements and actions could compromise personal or organisational integrity and reputation
- Make critical decisions to identify appropriate ethical behaviour when interacting with others in a variety of circumstances
- Refer and seek advice from relevant sources for issues beyond own professional competence
- Discuss, agree and resolve any ethical conflict

INTRODUCTION TO ETHICS

What are ethics?

ETHICS are a set of moral principles which guide behaviour.

Ethical values are assumptions and beliefs about what constitutes 'right' and 'wrong' behaviour.

Individuals have ethical values, often reflecting the beliefs of the families, cultures and educational environments in which they developed their ideas.

Organisations also have ethical values, based on the norms and standards of behaviour that their leaders believe will best help them express their identity and achieve their objectives. Some of these ethical values may be explicit: included in the organisation's mission statement, set out in Ethical Codes and Guidelines, or taught in employee training programmes. Other values may be part of the ORGANISATION CULTURE: 'the way we do things around here', the unwritten rules and customs of behaviour that develop over time as people find ways of working together.

Activity 1

Give some examples of the kinds of behaviour that were considered 'right' or 'wrong'

a) in your family;
b) in your national culture; and
c) in a particular organisation in which you have been employed.

WHY BEHAVE ETHICALLY?

The AAT's Guidelines on Professional Ethics (on which this Companion is substantially based) note that: 'the decisions you make in the everyday course of your professional lives can have real ethical implications.'

You must **print out a copy of the AAT's Guidelines on Professional Ethics** from the AAT's website (www.aat.org.uk) and read through it. Many of the tasks in your simulation will be based upon the principles in these Guidelines.

The Guidelines suggest several key reasons why an accounting technician should strive to behave ethically.

- Ethical issues may be a matter of **law and regulation**. You are expected to know and apply the laws of the country in which you live and work – as a basic minimum requirement for good practice. (It is sometimes said that 'the law is a floor': the lowest acceptable level of behaviour required to preserve the public interest and individual rights.)

student notes✍

- The **AAT** (like other professional bodies) requires its members to conduct themselves, and provide services to clients, according to certain professional and ethical standards. It does this, in part, to maintain its own **reputation and standing** – but this is also of benefit to its members and to the accounting profession as a whole.

- Professional and ethical behaviour protects the **public interest**. The accountancy profession sees itself as having duties to society as a whole – in addition to its specific obligations to employers and clients.

In more general terms, ethical behaviour is based on principles which are important to human life and society: respect for other people's rights, for example. Why behave ethically? Because ultimately, that's how organisations and societies survive.

FUNDAMENTAL ETHICAL PRINCIPLES

You might have your own ideas about what 'ethical behaviour' looks like – and these ideas will be shaped by your personal assumptions and values, and the values of the culture in which you operate (at work and in the country in which you live). However, there are certain basic or **'fundamental' principles** which underpin ethical behaviour in an accounting context.

- Integrity
- Objectivity
- Professional competence and due care
- Confidentiality
- Professional behaviour

Let's look at each of these briefly in turn. (We will be examining specific issues raised by these principles in later chapters.) **You need to be able to recognise and quote each of these fundamental principles**.

Integrity

'A member must be straightforward and honest in all professional and business relationships' (*AAT Guidelines*). On an obvious level, of course, this means not committing financial fraud – but it may also involve 'everyday' matters such as being open with clients about the limitations of your knowledge or competence, or carrying out work for your employer conscientiously and efficiently.

Activity 2

Give some examples of what you think 'integrity' might mean for you as an accounting technician, employed by a firm.

5

Objectivity

This is an extremely important principle for the accounting profession, because it protects the interests both of the parties directly affected by their services (clients, members of a company and so on) and of the general public (who rely on the accuracy of information and the integrity of financial systems).

OBJECTIVITY is the principle that all professional and business judgements should be made fairly:

- On the basis of an independent and intellectually honest appraisal of information

- Free from all forms of prejudice, bias and partiality

- Free from factors which might affect impartiality, such as pressure from a superior; financial interest in the outcome, a personal or professional relationship with one of the parties involved; or a conflict of interest (where one client stands to lose and another to gain by a particular disclosure).

In other words, 'a member must not allow bias, conflict of interest or undue influence of others to override professional or business judgements'. (*AAT Guidelines*)

What can you do to preserve objectivity? You should check that any perceived threat to your objectivity is offset by appropriate **safeguards**: your personal integrity and awareness; and the general safeguards provided by your professional environment (such as the likelihood of disciplinary action). You may need to apply additional safeguards in particular cases (for example, getting someone else to monitor your work).

However, if these safeguards are insufficient to offset the danger of your being (or even appearing to be) biased, you may need to refuse to act for a particular client in a particular matter.

Professional competence

Accountants have an obligation to their employers and clients to know what they are doing – and to do it right!

'A member has a continuing duy to maintain professional knowledge and skill at the level required to ensure that a client or employer receives competent professional service based on current developments in practice, legislation and techniques'. (*AAT Guidelines*)

You shouldn't **accept** an assignment which you don't have the competence to carry out to a satisfactory standard – unless you are sure that you will be able to get the help and advice you need to do so. And if you discover in the course of performing an assignment that you lack the knowledge or competence to complete it satisfactorily, you shouldn't **continue** without taking steps to get the help you need.

Activity 3

How do you think you can attain 'professional competence', as defined by the AAT? Think of your current programme of study – and what else might be required for you to perform accounting services to an acceptable standard.

In addition, once you have become a member of the profession, you need to **maintain** and **develop** your professional and technical competence, to keep pace with the demands which may be made on you in your work – and developments which may affect your work over time. This may mean:

- Regularly reviewing your practices against national and international standards, codes, regulations and legislation. Are you complying with the latest requirements?

- Continually upgrading your knowledge and skills in line with developments in accounting practices, requirements and techniques – and making sure that you don't get 'rusty' in the skills you have! (We will look at the AAT's recommendations for Continuing Professional Development [CPD] in chapter 3.)

Due care

DUE CARE is a legal concept which states that, having accepted an assignment, you have a contractual obligation to carry it out to the best of your ability, in the client's best interests, and within reasonable timescales (given the scope and nature of the assignment) – with proper regard for the technical and professional standards expected of you as a professional.

'A member must act diligently and in accordance with applicable technical and professional standards when providing professional services'. (*AAT Guidelines*)

As the expert in your field, you may often deal with clients who have little knowledge of accounting or taxation matters. This puts you in a position of power, which must never be abused by carrying out your assignment in a negligent or 'careless' way.

Confidentiality

CONFIDENTIALITY is an important value in many relationships, both personal and legal. You need to respect the confidentiality of information acquired as a result of professional and business relationships (for reasons which we will discuss in detail later). This means that you will not **use** it, or **disclose** it to others, unless:

- You have **specific** and **'proper' authorisation** to do so by the client or employer.

- You are legally or professionally **entitled** or *obliged* to do so.

In addition, 'confidential information acquired as a result of professional and business relationships must not be used for the personal advantage of the member or third parties'. (*AAT Guidelines*)

We will look mainly at the confidentiality of *financial* information from the point of view of providing professional services. It is also worth being aware that personal information shared with you by clients and colleagues at work should be regarded as confidential – unless you are told otherwise: this is an important basis for trust in any working relationship.

Activity 4

Your manager asks you to tell a client about the financial problems being experienced by another client, as a useful warning to them about the need for effective financial controls. What ethical issues does this raise?

Professional behaviour

Again, you'll have your own ideas about what 'being professional' means, but in a technical sense, it involves behaving in a way that maintains or enhances the reputation of your profession: bringing it credit – not discredit. 'A member must comply with relevant laws and regulations and avoid any action that brings a profession in disrepute'. (*AAT Guidelines*)

One key aspect of this is **courtesy**, for example. As a professional, you should behave with courtesy and consideration towards anyone with whom you come into contact in the course of your work and indeed in your personal life.

HOW IT WORKS

Now that we've considered the fundamental principles in general, let's consider some typical scenarios in which they might be helpful.

You are an accounting technician employed by a large firm of chartered accounts, Belgiorno Bellman & Partners, in their office in Birmingham, England. You have responsibility for several clients, reporting to a partner who oversees your work, but you are the main contact for the clients.

In the course of your working week, you notice or are involved in the following incidents. In each case, we will identify the ethical issues they present, in line with the basic principles discussed so far.

Incident one

You have to complete your time sheet for the week. You inadvertently forgot to note your hours on Monday, and cannot now remember what time you put in working for which clients. 'Just average out the hours,' says a colleague. 'That's what everyone does.'

There is an **integrity** issue here. Inaccuracy may result in time being charged to the wrong client, who will be billed for work that hasn't in fact been done. The fact that 'everyone does it' (even if true) doesn't make it right: you need to make your own decision.

Incident two

You have received a letter from an estate agent, requesting financial information about one of your individual clients, who is applying to rent a property. The information is needed as soon as possible, by fax or e-mail, in order to secure approval for the client.

There is a **confidentiality** issue here. You need the client's authority to disclose the information: you may also need to confirm the identity of the person making the request. You should also take steps to protect the confidentiality of the information when you send it: for example, not using fax or e-mail (which can be intercepted) and stating clearly that the information is confidential.

Incident three

While out to lunch, you run into a client at the sandwich bar. In conversation, she tells you that she expects to inherit from a recently deceased uncle, and asks you how she will be affected by inheritance tax, capital gains tax and other matters – which you have not dealt with, in detail, for some years.

There are issues of **due care** and **competence** here. Any answer you give on the spot would risk being incomplete, inaccurate or out-of-date – with potentially serious consequences, if the client relies and acts on your reply. You should make an appointment to discuss the matter properly, after you've done some research.

Incident four

One of your clients, a travel agent, is so pleased with the amount of tax you saved him this year that he offers you a free weekend break in a luxury hotel, just as a 'thank you'.

There is an **objectivity** issue here. The gift is of significant value. Given that the client has paid for your tax advice, an observer might be entitled to wonder what 'special favours' deserve this extra reward – and/or how such a gift may bias you in the client's favour in future.

Incident five

You have just taken over a client from another firm. Some time ago, you requested the previous accountants to send over the client's books and records. They didn't. Each time you call to chase up the request, they claim not to have received it, or that the person dealing with the matter is out. Meanwhile, it appears that they are telling the client that you have failed to contact them. Finally, in a conference call with the client present, they swear at you and call you a 'client stealer'.

This is simply **unprofessional behaviour** by the other accountants. (You may consider reporting the matter to their professional body!)

> ## Signpost
>
> See the *AAT Ethical Guidelines*:
>
> - **Section 100**: Fundamental principles
> - **Section 110**: Integrity
> - **Section 120**: Objectivity
> - **Section 130**: Professional competence and due care
> - **Section 140**: Confidentiality
> - **Section 150**: Professional behaviour

IDENTIFYING APPROPRIATE ETHICAL BEHAVIOURS

Of course, the principles outlined above aren't enough in themselves to tell you what the 'right thing to do' is in every specific situation you may encounter! (Otherwise, we could finish our Course Companion right here.) But they do provide useful **guidelines** for decision-making. If a course of action looks like violating any of these principles – whatever the specific circumstances – that course of action will be worth questioning.

Unfortunately, ethical issues are seldom clear-cut. You may often encounter situations where a course of action appears to be on the 'borderline' between ethical (or at least widely accepted) and unethical. One notorious 'grey' area is the receiving of business gifts, especially in cross-cultural contexts, where cultural norms and expectations may differ.

How do you know which is the 'right' course of action in a given situation or interaction?

Ethics and the law

Generally speaking, ethical conduct is legal conduct. (There are examples of conduct which some people may want to identify as illegal-but-ethical, but they shouldn't apply to you as an Accounting Technician!) You need to comply with the law, encourage your colleagues and employers (where relevant) to comply with the law – and advise your clients to comply with the law.

You will have encountered a range of legal provisions in your AAT studies and workplace experience: be aware that these are all potentially relevant to professional ethics, insofar as they affect your behaviour and reputation as an accounting technician! (We will look at some aspects of this in chapter 4.)

Activity 5

Give five examples of laws which affect (or should affect) your everyday behaviour at work – not necessarily in the way you perform your accounting duties.

Critical decision-making on ethical issues

First of all, consider the application of available **legal** and **ethical guidelines** in the particular situation you are facing.

- How might the principles apply?

- Are there examples (or legal precedents) which might act as a template?

If the situation is still unclear, critical decision-making may be required. Two sets of ideas may be useful in helping you to reach a reasoned conclusion that will withstand later scrutiny.

- **Consider the consequences.** What will be the effects of the course of action – on you and others? An action may have both positive and negative impacts, or may affect some people positively and others negatively. However, a course of action which is likely to have an unacceptably high cost for any of the parties concerned may be said to be unethical.

A basic test is to consider: would you feel comfortable and confident, if you had to defend your decision or action before a court, or in the Press, or to a moral/spiritual adviser you admire? If not, this may be an indication that, deep down, you know that it is potentially unethical.

■ **Consider your obligations.** What do you 'owe' other people in the situation? Some obligations are clearly set out in contracts (eg with employers and clients) – but we also, arguably, have a general 'duty' to treat others fairly and humanely.

A basic test (using the 'golden rule' which is part of all major ethical systems) is to consider: would you want to be on the receiving end of whatever action you are about to take? If not, this may be an indication that it is potentially unethical.

So the key questions are:

a) Is it legal and in line with company policy and professional guidelines?

b) How will it make me feel about myself?

c) Is it balanced and fair to all concerned, so that there are no 'losers' by it?

There are also outside sources of advice and guidance, which you may choose to access – but it is important to observe the requirement for confidentiality until you are sure that the situation is such that you have a right and duty to disclose it. Confidentiality is another key principle meaning that you do not disclose information given to you in the 'confidence' it will not be disclosed.

Getting help with ethical concerns and dilemmas

If you are employed by an organisation, any matter of ethical concern – whether or not it is explicitly addressed in the AAT's Ethical Guidelines – should be raised with your immediate supervisor, if possible.

However, if the ethical issue concerns the organisation, or if you are self-employed, you may need to seek independent advice – within the requirements for professional confidentiality.

■ Seek **independent legal advice** (particularly if there are potential legal consequences to your actions – and even more particularly if you are practising outside the country or culture with which you are familiar). Legal advisers are also bound by professional confidentiality, so this offers protection to you and the others involved in the situation. (Talking to a spouse, friend or colleague doesn't!)

- If you are still in doubt about the proper course of action, you can contact the **AAT's Ethics Advice line** (e-mail: ethics@aat.org.uk), presenting all the relevant facts.

Written records should be kept of any such discussions and meetings (as for other forms of conflict resolution at work), to ensure that there is evidence of the advice you have received. This will help protect you in any legal proceedings that may result: if your subsequent conduct is prosecuted, for example – or if you are unfairly victimised or dismissed for taking a stand on the issue.

HOW IT WORKS

Back at Belgiorno Bellman, you have been asked by the partner to whom you report, Sheila Branxholme, to sit in and take notes as she interviews an applicant for the post of receptionist with the firm.

In the course of the interview, your attention is drawn to the following aspects of the discussion.

- Sheila, having learned that the candidate has three small children, asks lots of questions about her plans to have more children and her childcare arrangements. When the candidate, in return, asks about the firm's family-friendly working policies, you notice that Sheila omits to mention the childcare assistance which you know is available.

- The candidate reveals that the family depends mainly on income from her husband's job at a local electrical goods manufacturer. As it happens, this company is one of your clients – and you are aware of its plans to shut down the local plant over the coming year.

- The candidate left her previous employers because they continued to employ a popular and successful member of their sales staff who had sexually harassed her and another female employee. This firm is another client of Belgiorno Bellman.

After the candidate has left, Sheila looks across at you and rolls her eyes and says: 'Just lose those notes, will you?'

What are the ethical issues raised here, and how will you decide what (if anything) to do about them?

- Sheila's focus on family responsibilities may be construed as sexual discrimination under UK law – unless she asks the same questions of any men she interviews for the job.

- Giving incomplete information about the organisation might be more significantly unethical if its effect was to mislead someone into taking employment under false pretences. In this case, not much harm is being done, as the candidate is merely being influenced against accepting a job that she probably won't be offered anyway.

■ You may feel sorry for the family, who are unaware that the husband will soon lose his job. But this is a fact of economic life – and you have the overriding duty not to disclose what you know about the client's plans.

■ The behaviour of the candidate's previous employer is unethical (and possibly illegal). But you have come by the information indirectly – and is it anything to do with you? It would certainly be in your client's best interests not to risk legal claims against them.

■ Sheila's request to you to 'lose the notes' is ambiguous. It sounds unethical – whether as a suggestion of prejudice against the candidate, or as a way of dodging responsibility for the ethical issues raised.

So what might you do? First you might decide to clarify exactly what Sheila meant: this would clear up any misunderstanding, and highlight the ethical issues more clearly. It might also be possible to draw her attention (respectfully) to the risks of her interview questions being construed as discrimination.

Other than this, it may not be your place to do much more – although you may choose to advise your clients of the ethical and legal considerations that have come to your attention: the need to be socially responsible in notifying employees as early as possible of impending redundancies; and the need for consistency, fairness and compliance in regard to disciplinary issues (such as sexual harassment).

THE CONCEPTUAL FRAMEWORK

It is impossible to give guidelines on every possible situation that might arise in the course of your work which might cause a conflict with the fundamental ethical principles. The AAT's *Ethical Guidelines* therefore seek to set out a basic **problem solving procedure** which you can use in any situation, to give yourself the best chance of complying with the principles.

The basic procedure (or 'conceptual framework') is as follows.

■ Identify where these may be a threat to a fundamental principle.

■ **Evaluate the threat**: how serious is it?

■ For any threat that is not clearly insignificant (that is, for any serious threat), **apply safeguards** that will eliminate the threat or reduce it to an acceptable level (so that compliance with the fundamental principle is not compromised).

- If safeguards cannot be applied, **decline or discontinue** the specific action or professional service involved, or where necessary, **resign** from the client (if you are a member in practice) or the employing organisation (if you are a member in business).

Threats

Many of the threats which may create a risk of compromising on the fundamental principles will fall into one of the following categories.

- **Self-interest threats**. You (or those closely connected to you) are financially involved, or stand to gain financially, from a situation. For example, you may have a significant financial stake (such as shares) in a client company, and might therefore be reluctant to take action that would have an adverse effect on the value of these shares. Another example would be if you were offered a bribe or inducement to do something (or not to do something).

- **Self-review threats**. You have been involved in decisions or actions (such as the preparation of accounts) which you are being asked to review, evaluate or report on. For example, you might be asked to prepare financial statements, when you have also been involved in maintaining accounting records or doing valuations. The risk is that you will be biased (whether knowingly or not) in your own favour – and there will be no genuine objective check on the work or decision.

- **Familiarity threats**. You have built up an emotional commitment to, or trust in, a client, employer or third party, and may therefore be so sympathetic to their interests that you will be unable to be wholly objective – or may be tempted to protect or enhance their interests in some way. For example, you may be asked to advise a client with whom you have a family connection, or evaluate the work of a colleague who is also a close friend.

- **Intimidation threats**. You are threatened or pressured (or you *feel* threatened or pressured) by others to take a particular action, or not to take it. For example, you feel you will lose your job if you don't report favourably on your employer.

- **Advocacy threats**. You have strong views in support of a client, particularly in a conflict situation. The risk is that, since you have strongly promoted that position or opinion, people will have difficulty in believing that you are objective about the matter or the party you have supported. For example, you might stand up for client or employer in a court case, giving the impression that you are 'on their side'.

Safeguards

There are two broad categories of safeguards that you might use to reduce or eliminate threats.

- **Safeguards created by the profession and/or legislation and regulation**. Legal rules and professional codes are specifically designed to support ethical behaviour: a partial solution is therefore to comply with the rules! Potential safeguards include:

    - Education and training, as a requirement for entry into (and continuing development within) the profession. (This is a safeguard because it helps you make the right decisions.)

    - Corporate governance regulations (eg on financial reporting)

    - Professional standards (and related monitoring and disciplinary procedures)

    - Third-party review of financial reports and returns produced by members (eg the auditing of accounts)

- **Safeguards in the work environment**, which increase the likelihood of identifying or deterring unethical behaviour, include:

    - Quality controls, and internal audits of quality controls

    - Mechanisms to empower and protect staff who raise ethical concerns ('whistleblowers')

    - Involvement of, or consultation with, independent third parties (eg non executive directors or regulatory bodies)

    - Rotation of personnel to avoid increasing familiarity and opportunities for collusion in fraud

    - Opportunities to discuss ethical dilemmas (eg with an ethics officer, committee or forum)

We will look at more specific threats and safeguards, applicable in different situations, as we cover particular scenarios.

> ## Signpost
>
> See the *AAT Ethical Guidelines*:
>
> - **Section 100**: Conceptual framework approach (100.5 – 100.9)
> - **Section 100**: Threats and safeguards (100.10 – 100.15)

DEALING WITH ETHICAL CONFLICTS

What is an ethical conflict?

It is almost inevitable that at some time in your career, you will meet a situation which presents some kind of ethical dilemma or conflict, where:

- Two ethical values or requirements seem to be incompatible: eg you have the duty to disclose unethical conduct that has come to your attention – but also the duty of professional confidentiality.

- Two sets of demands and obligations seem to be incompatible ('conflicting loyalties'): eg if an employer or client asks you to break the ethical guidelines of your profession: falsifying a record; making a misleading statement; or supplying information 'recklessly', without being in a position to know whether or not it is true. (We will deal with such conflicts more specifically in chapter 4.) Such situations may be particularly acute if you are put under pressure to do the wrong thing by an overbearing supervisor, or by a valued client, friend or relation.

Note that not everyone thinks alike on all ethical matters! It is quite possible that a fellow professional, or a work colleague, will honestly disagree with you about what constitutes an ethical or unethical course of action: this doesn't necessarily mean that you have an 'ethical conflict', or that you have to report and formally resolve the matter!

The kind of genuine ethical conflict which must be resolved is one which puts you in a position where you are being asked or required to take – or be party to – action which you feel may be unethical.

Activity 6

From what you know so far, would you have an ethical conflict if you suspected that a client had supplied information on a tax return without checking the details or having supporting documentation to hand?

Resolving ethical conflicts

If you are asked, instructed or encouraged to take a course of action which is illegal, or unethical by the standards of your profession, you are **entitled** and **required** to refuse.

This can lead to interpersonal – and perhaps even legal – conflict.

Some issues may be 'cleared up' by informal discussion: they may be based on a misunderstanding, or ignorance – or the belief that no-one knows what

student notes✍

is going on! Your first aim will be to persuade the relevant parties not to take (or persist in) the unethical course of action.

If informal discussion (usually involving the party most nearly involved, or your immediate supervisor) doesn't work, and the issue is significant, more formal avenues may be pursued.

Within an **organisation** (for members in business), there may be established procedures for resolving ethical issues and conflicts with colleagues or superiors, such as those for dealing with **grievances**. If this does not produce a satisfactory result, the problem should be discussed with the next level up in the management hierarchy, and/or arbitrators such as an Ethics Committee or those in charge of corporate governance (eg the board of directors or audit committee). If a conflict still exists after all internal avenues to resolution have been explored, the accountant may have no alternative but to resign. (We will discuss these matters in more detail in chapter 4.)

Similarly, in a **self-employed** situation (for members in practice), if a client requests or instructs you to take a course of action which is unethical or illegal, you are entitled and required to refuse. The request may be made in ignorance and good faith – and you should attempt to explain the technical, legal and ethical principles that apply. If the client continues to insist, or refuses to change his or her own unethical conduct (where this reflects on you as his or her agent or adviser), you should simply cease to act for that client.

If the issue is unresolved, even if you have taken steps to protect your own integrity and reputation by resigning or ceasing to act, you may still have a duty to report illegal or unethical conduct to relevant authorities. This is a tricky area, because of the competing duty of confidentiality: we will look at it in detail in later chapters.

HOW IT WORKS

You have voiced your unease about the inaccuracy of the section's time sheets to Sheila. 'Forget it,' she says. 'The clients are still getting good value for money one way or another. Do you think the partners waste time tying down every hour that goes astray here or there? You worry too much.'

This is an ethical conflict, if you choose to pursue the matter (as compromising your professional ethics) and Sheila insists that you let the matter drop. The culture of Belgiorno Bellman, from the top down, is clearly unsympathetic to what are seen as 'minor' ethical concerns. You may have to go to the Ethics Committee (which should include impartial members), or get independent advice (from the AAT or a legal adviser) as to whether or how to take the matter further.

Meanwhile, you have sat in on another interview for the post of receptionist. This candidate, who is very keen and is currently working for another firm of chartered accountants in the city, appears to be the perfect person for the job. As Sheila is bringing the interview to a close, the candidate says: 'By the way, I thought you might like to see the kind of systems I've got experience with. Here's a copy, on disc, of our Contacts Management software.' Sheila accepts the disc.

After the interview, you tell Sheila that you are not comfortable about this. She says that although it is, technically, a breach of copyright, she will destroy the disk after looking over it: this is probably within the definition of 'fair dealing'.

You suspect, however, that the candidate has actually handed her a competing firm's (highly confidential) client/contact list. This would clearly be unethical to accept, let alone use. Does Sheila have similar suspicions, or is she acting in ignorance? Did the candidate offer the disc in good faith – or as an incentive to influence the selection decision? You should state your concerns clearly to Sheila about this. If Sheila knowingly takes advantage of unethically-obtained information, and expects you to be silent about it, you are being made party to an unethical course of action: this is a serious ethical conflict, and you should get confidential independent advice on how to deal with it.

Signpost

See the *AAT Ethical Guidelines*:

- **Section 100**: Ethical conflict resolution (100.16 – 100.21)

CHAPTER OVERVIEW

- Ethical values are assumptions and beliefs about what constitutes 'right' and 'wrong' behaviour. Individuals, families, national cultures and organisation cultures all develop ethical values and norms.

- Ethical behaviour is necessary to comply with law and regulation; to protect the public interest; to protect the reputation and standing of a professional body and its members; and to enable people to live and work together in society.

- Fundamental ethical principles in an accounting context are:

  - Integrity
  - Objectivity
  - Professional and technical competence
  - Due care
  - Confidentiality and
  - Professional behaviour

KEY WORDS

Ethics are a set of moral principles which guide behaviour.

Organisation culture is 'the way we do things around here'.

Objectivity means making a decision fairly and with intellectual honesty, on the basis of all relevant considerations – and no irrelevant considerations.

Confidentiality means not using or disclosing information given 'in confidence' that you will keep it to yourself.

Due care is a legal obligation to carry out work competently and carefully, with regard for technical and professional standards.

- The ethical course of action, in a given situation or interaction, may be determined with regard to:

  - Available ethical/legal guidelines and examples/precedents
  - The consequences of the action for all parties involved
  - The obligations you owe to all parties involved
  - Advice and guidance from a superior, solicitor or the AAT.

- Significant ethical conflict may occur if you are required (by a client or employer) to perform, or be party to, unethical or illegal action. Conflict resolution or grievance procedures should be pursued to resolve the issue. As a last resort, it may be necessary to cease to act for a client, or to resign from an employing organisation, rather than breach professional ethics.

HOW MUCH HAVE YOU LEARNED?

1   Only individuals can have 'ethical values'. True or false?

2   Why does the AAT have an interest in whether its members behave ethically or not?

3   Give three examples of factors which might (or might be thought to) affect the objectivity and independence of providers of professional accounting services.

4   A client for whom you are preparing a tax return asks you a technical question about VAT, which you are not sure you are able to answer correctly. 'You are supposed to be a tax specialist, aren't you?' says the client. 'I need an answer now.'

What ethical issues are raised by this scenario, and what should you do?

5   One of your clients is a civil engineer which has asked your advice in regard to setting up financial controls for a major road-building project, which the firm have been invited to tender for. The project is to build a by-pass, diverting traffic away from the historic centre of the town in which you operate. The project has not yet been announced to the Press or public, although development plans have been posted at the Town Planning office.

Several of your other clients will be affected by the project, if it goes ahead. One is a petrol station, whose business will be severely affected by the by-pass, losing the majority of its drive-past customers. Another is a café, and you anticipate that it will benefit from the improved ambience: there is a rumour that the council is planning a pedestrian precinct, which will increase its walk-in trade. This will be very timely, as the café has not been doing well, and the owners were shortly planning to sell the business.

Your sister has just been given the position of manager of the petrol station.

Meanwhile, the other big winners in the by-pass project are the construction firm which will be employed by the civil engineers. 'I'd buy shares in that company, if I were you,' joked the civil engineer as he left your office.

What ethical issues are raised by this scenario, and what should you do?

6   Outline the four steps of the problem-solving methodology or 'conceptual framework' for ethical conduct.

chapter 2:
IDENTIFYING ETHICAL ISSUES

chapter coverage 📖

In this chapter, we highlight some professional work situations which specifically raise issues of compliance or the need for critical decision-making about the ethical course of action. The AAT's assessment criteria for Unit 32 state clearly that it is not always possible to come up with a 'correct' approach to ethical issues: what is important is that students demonstrate an understanding of when there is an ethical issue that needs to be considered, and use the conceptual framework to propose an appropriate course of action.

Ethical issues may be raised by your own personal values, or those of your employing organisation, or – more clearly – by organisational or professional ethical guidelines, statutory requirements or contractual obligations towards clients and others.

The topics we shall cover are:

✍ Fraud

✍ Independence and objectivity

✍ Confidentiality

✍ Contractual obligations

✍ Preparing financial statements

✍ Taxation services

✍ Internal audit

Knowledge and understanding

- The guidelines of your professional body
- A principle-based approach to professional ethics
- Legal considerations

Performance criteria – Element 32.1

- Highlight situations within professional work that require objectivity and fairness, and where judgements and actions could compromise personal or organisational integrity and reputation

- Recognise and explain why certain types of information should be regarded as confidential

- Identify circumstances when it would be appropriate to disclose confidential information

- Identify the key issues which ensure professional services are performed within the scope of professional ethics guidance

- Describe the types of contractual obligations you would have in providing services to clients, to include due care and carrying out assignments within a reasonable time scale

FRAUD

There is no precise legal definition of FRAUD, but it may generally be defined as 'deprivation by deceit'.

In a corporate context, fraud can fall into one of two main categories:

Category	Comment
Removal of funds or assets from a business	The most obvious example of this is outright theft, either of cash or of other assets. However, this form of fraud also encompasses more subtle measures, such as the overstatement of expenses claims.
Intentional misrepresentation of the financial position of the business	This includes the omission or misrecording of the company's accounting records: overstating profits, falsifying sales invoices and so on.

Let's consider some practical examples within each category. This isn't an exhaustive list of examples: every business is unique in its own way and offers different opportunities for fraud to be committed! You need to be able to think critically about a situation and identify for yourself areas and ways in which frauds could be occurring.

Activity 1

How might the ability to identify where fraud may be occurring be relevant to your work as an accounting technician?

Removal of funds or assets from a business

Theft of cash or stock. Employees with access to cash (such as petty cash) may be tempted to steal: small amounts taken at intervals may easily go unnoticed. Similarly, employees may pilfer stock (such as stationery or materials). Such fraud tends to be too insignificant to have any serious impact on results or long-term performance – but it is still fraud!

Payroll fraud. Employees may falsify their timesheets, for example, by claiming overtime for hours which they didn't really work.

Members of the payroll department may have the opportunity deliberately to miscalculate selected payslips (eg applying an inflated rate of pay) or even to add fictitious staff members to the payroll list (pocketing the pay themselves).

Teeming and lading. The sales ledger clerk steals cash or cheque receipts and conceals the theft by setting subsequent receipts against the outstanding debt.

Collusion with customers. Employees may collude with customers to defraud the business by manipulating prices or the quality or quantity of goods despatched. For example, a sales manager may reduce the price charged to a customer in return for a cut of the saving, or may write off a debt in return for a financial incentive.

Collusion with suppliers. Staff may collude with suppliers, who issue invoices for larger quantities of goods than were actually delivered, splitting the additional payments between the parties involved.

Misuse of assets. Misuse of pension funds, for example, has been a high-profile form of corporate fraud in recent years. Ailing companies may raid the pension fund to use as collateral in obtaining loan finance, or for many other reasons. More subtly, a company may manipulate the book value of assets: over-depreciating assets (eg a company car) for sale to employees so that they pay below-market value for them; or over-valuing assets transferred to the pension fund.

Intentional misrepresentation of the financial position of the business

The financial statements of a business are supposed to give a 'true and fair' view of its financial situation. The following are examples of fraud where the intention is to overstate profits. (By reversing the logic, you can also use them as examples of methods for understating profits…)

Over-valuation of stock. Stock is a particularly attractive area for management wishing to inflate net assets artificially. Stock records may be manipulated (eg by 'miscounting' stock items). Alternatively, deliveries to customers and returns to suppliers may simply be omitted from the records.

Bad debts. Aged debtors who are obviously not going to pay should be written off: however, by not enforcing this policy, management can avoid the negative effects it would have on profits and net assets.

Fictitious sales. Inflated sales figures can be achieved by generating false invoices, overcharging customers for goods or services, or (perhaps more creatively) selling goods to friends (with a promise of buying them back at a later date!)

Manipulating year-end. Cut-off dates provide management with opportunities for window-dressing the financial statements. Sales made just before year end can be deliberately over-invoiced and credit notes issued with an apology at the start of the new year – enhancing turnover and profit during the year just ended! (Delaying the recording of pre-year-end purchases of goods not yet delivered can achieve the same objective.)

Understating expenses. Clearly, failure to record all expenses accurately will inflate the reported profit figure. More subtly, depreciation figures (a form of expense) may be manipulated: applying incorrect rates to understate depreciation, for example, will result in a higher profit and a higher net book value, giving a more favourable impression of financial health.

Activity 2

Try to think of reasons why someone might want to:

a)   artificially enhance the results of a business.
b)   under-report the results of a business.

HOW IT WORKS

You are preparing quarterly management accounts for your café client, and come across the following items, which seem to you to be suspicious.

■   There is an invoice, filed under 'fixtures and fittings', which appears to be for a lounge suite and TV cabinet.

■   The office catering service, which takes sandwiches and snacks round local businesses for sale to employees, appears to have very low takings over the last two months, compared to other periods. When you query this, the owner simply says that 'business was slow' – but something in the way this is said makes you think this wasn't in fact the case.

These items are suspicious, even though you have no proof of attempted fraud. It look as though the café owners are trying to reduce their tax liability by:

■   Passing off a personal/home purchase as a business expense

■   Avoiding disclosing all income from the catering service (where receipts are in cash)

Without evidence, you decide to query the items with the owners: there may be a simple mistake or misunderstanding, which can be cleared up (eg by not reflecting the furniture bill in the accounts of the café).

You may ask the café owners for an assurance (in writing) that only business items are included in the accounts and that all income has been disclosed: this should cover you – and perhaps deter them from further attempts.

Why is fraud a bad thing?

The **removal of funds** or **assets** from a business has immediate financial implications for an organisation. Profits are lower than they should be: the business has less cash or fewer assets, weakening the net asset position – and potentially lowering returns to shareholders. The long term effects of significant fraud are even more serious: the reduction in working capital makes it more difficult for the company to operate effectively, and may ultimately cause it to collapse (as in the case of Barings Bank, for example).

Intentional misrepresentation of the financial position of the business likewise has potentially serious consequences.

- If results are **overstated**, there may be shortfalls in working capital – making day-to-day activities more difficult to perform effectively. Incorrect decisions will be made, based on inaccurate knowledge of the available resources.

- If results are **understated**, returns to investors may be reduced unnecessarily; access to loan finance may be restricted. If the company is quoted on the stock exchange, the share price might fall – and the negative publicity may damage the business.

- The effects of fraudulent activities can affect STAKEHOLDERS in the organisation, if the financial statements upon which they rely are misrepresentations of the truth. For example, investors may not get the returns they expect; suppliers may extend credit without adequate security.

Fraud of any kind also has **legal consequences**. Depending on the scale and seriousness of the fraud, offenders may be open to disciplinary action (including dismissal) by their employer – and potentially legal action leading to imprisonment.

INDEPENDENCE AND OBJECTIVITY

AAT members need to maintain independence, in order to protect the integrity of their professional services. This applies both to:

- **Being independent.** The AAT Guidelines refer to 'independence of mind' (objectivity) as the ability to put aside all considerations which are not relevant to the decision or task in hand – free from bias, prejudice or partiality

- **Being seen to be independent** ('*independence in appearance*'): the ability to **demonstrate** independence by avoiding situations which would cause a reasonable and informed observer to question your ability to be objective. Examples include clear **threats to objectivity** such as a personal financial interest in the outcome; a personal relationship with the client; or managerial/operational involvement in activities being reviewed. (Specific threats will be examined, as they apply to the activities of members in business and members in practice, in chapters 4 and 5.)

Perhaps the most important way of maintaining independence is to be aware that you may be exposed to influences, pressures and other threats to your objectivity.

If you are aware of these pressures, you can analyse them and judge whether there are sufficient **safeguards** in place to reduce the risk of compromise to acceptable levels.

General safeguards include:

- Your own strength of character and professionalism, which enable you to stand up to pressure from a supervisor or client and do the right thing

- Your awareness of your legal accountability, and potential penalties under the law

- Your awareness of your professional accountability, and disciplinary action that may be taken against you by your professional body

- Your awareness of potential negative impact on your professional reputation (and future livelihood)

Activity 3

a) What is 'independence in appearance' – and why is it important?

b) Give three examples of situations where your 'independence in appearance' may be threatened.

Gifts and hospitality

One of the key threats to objectivity (and the appearance of objectivity) is accepting gifts, services, favours or hospitality from parties who may have an interest in the outcome of your work:

- A client

- A work colleague

- Any party with a current or proposed contractual relationship with your employing organisation: contractors, suppliers and so on.

These may be (or may be seen as) an attempt to influence the objectivity of your decisions, or to make you do or not do something. You don't personally have to be the intended recipient: gifts to your spouse or dependent children are assumed to be equally compromising.

(Note also that if you offer gifts, favours or hospitality, this may be seen as an attempt unethically to influence others.)

Does this mean that you can't accept a bottle of wine at Christmas, or a calendar from a supplier? No. The gift needs to be **significant enough** that it could be reasonably perceived, by person who has all the facts, as likely to influence your judgement.

Activity 4

You are invited to attend the Ashes Test Match at Lords Cricket Ground, London, in the corporate hospitality box of a consultancy firm that is bidding for the contract to design your company's new computer system. Is this an ethical issue for you?

Anti-corruption legislation

If you are employed by a public body in the UK (including government and local authorities), the acceptance of gifts may also be illegal under UK anti-corruption legislation.

- **The Public Bodies Corrupt Practices Act 1889** makes the active or passive bribery of a member or officer of a public body a criminal offence. 'A person may not corruptly solicit, or receive, or agree to receive … any gift, loan, fee, reward or advantage as an inducement to, or reward for, doing or forbearing to do anything in respect of any matter or transaction… in which the public body is concerned.'

  There are severe penalties for offences, including imprisonment, heavy fines, loss of office and prevention from taking public office in future.

- **The Prevention of Corruption Act 1906** prohibits agents (whether in the public or private sector) from corruptly soliciting, accepting or agreeing to accept a gift or consideration which would influence his actions or impartiality in relation to his principal's affairs or business.

  It is also an offence knowingly to give an agent (or for an agent knowingly to use) a receipt, account or other document which contains significant falsehoods, errors or omissions, with the intention of misleading his principal.

- **The Prevention of Corruption Act 1916** creates a 'presumption of corruption' relating to the above two Acts. In other words, if it can be proved that money, gifts or other considerations:

  - have been given to a person employed by a public body

  - by a person (or agent of a person) holding or seeking to obtain a contract from the public body

  it will be assumed that it was given and received corruptly as an inducement or reward – unless it can be proved otherwise.

Additional requirements were added under UK **Anti-Terrorism**, **Crime** and **Security** legislation:

- To cover public officials and agents outside the UK. (So you can't bribe foreign judges, MPs or ministers!)

- To allow bribery and corruption offences committed abroad by UK nationals and bodies (incorporated under UK law) to be prosecuted in the UK.

Anti-corruption measures are currently the topic of debate by the European Union and the OECD, and there may be amendments to the UK legislation over the next few years. (One example of your need to stay alert for new requirements, as part of your continuing professional development.)

HOW IT WORKS

Your petrol station client has now got wind of the proposed by-pass scheme, and its owners have decided to sell the land to a property developer and buy a similar franchise elsewhere.

Unfortunately, conflict has arisen between the owners, as to the distribution of the assets and liabilities from the sale. You have been asked to mediate between the two men – one of whom you went to school with and have always got on well with, and the other of whom you haven't dealt with much.

In the eyes of any informed observer, there is a threat to your objectivity in mediating between the interests of the two men, because of your closer relationship with one of them. Having discussed the matter with your partner, Sheila, you decide that your professional standards – and the fact that you have alerted Sheila to the potential problem – are still a sufficient safeguard, and you will be able to be objective.

The following day, however, you receive a visit from the old school friend, who brings you a handsome pot plant for your office (as a 'thank you' for your help) and tells you that he has been headhunted by a large local company, which he happens to know is looking for a new firm of accountants.

The small gift is insufficient to threaten your objectivity – but the implied recommendation to a major new client (and the fees arising from it) would appear to be an inducement to keep this client happy – possibly at the expense of his partner. After further discussion with Sheila, you recommend both partners to seek another mediator in their dispute.

Meanwhile, the clients have also asked you to prepare a declaration on the accuracy of the valuation of their property, for any legal proceedings that may ensue. The original valuation was done by Belgiorno Bellman. Since you may be seen to be biased towards approving your firm's conclusions, you decline the assignment.

student notes

→ **Signpost**

See the *AAT Ethical Guidelines*:

■   **Section 350**: Inducements (for members in business)
■   **Section 260**: Gifts and Hospitality (for members in practice)

CONFIDENTIALITY

As an accountant, you are likely to have access to a great deal of information about the financial affairs of your clients (or your employers and their clients) which would not, in the normal course of business, be disclosed to the public.

All information you receive through your work as an accountant should be regarded as confidential: that is, given in trust (or confidence) that it will not be shared or disclosed.

■   Information shared with the explicit proviso that it be kept private and confidential (as stated in a contract or verbal agreement).

■   Information shared within a professional/client relationship (eg with an accountant or solicitor) which is regarded as a relationship of 'trust and confidence' under the law.

■   Information that is restricted or classified within an organisation's information system (eg marked 'private', 'confidential' or 'for authorised individuals only').

■   Information protected by data protection and personal privacy law (eg in the UK, personal data held by organisations, and personal medical data of employees).

■   Information which could be used against the interests of the organisation or an individual.

Activity 5

Give some examples of information which, if disclosed, could be used against the interests of

a) an organisation and
b) an individual.

The duty of confidentiality

The AAT Guidelines state clearly that 'members have an obligation to respect the confidentiality of information about a client's or employer's affairs, or the affairs of clients of employers, acquired in the course of professional work'.

This may seem obvious, but it extends more widely than you may think.

- It applies even after the assignment, or the contractual relationship with the client or employer is over. (In other words, you need to respect the confidentiality of information about former clients and ex-employers too…)

- It applies not just to you, but to any staff under your authority, and any people you ask for advice or assistance. (It is up to you to ensure that they keep any information you share with them confidential too…)

What does 'respecting confidence' mean?

a) Not disclosing the information to other persons.

b) Not using (or even appearing to use) the information for your own personal advantage or that of someone else.

When *can* you disclose confidential information?

You are permitted to disclose confidential information in three specific sets of circumstances.

1) **When you are properly authorised to do so**

   The client or employer may legitimately authorise you to disclose the information. (Even so, you need to consider the effect of disclosure: will it be in the best interests of all the parties involved in the matter?)

2) **When you have a professional duty to do so**

   You are entitled to disclose information if it is necessary to do so in order to perform your work properly, according to the technical standards and ethical requirements of the profession.

   You also have a duty to disclose information if asked to do so by the AAT or another regulatory body, as part of an ethical or disciplinary investigation into your conduct (or the conduct of your employer or client).

3) **When you have a legal duty to do so**

   UK law requires you to:

   a) Produce documents or give evidence if asked to do so by a court of law, in the course of **legal proceedings** against you, or your client or employer.

   b) Disclose certain information to bodies which have **statutory powers** to demand the information, such as HM Revenue and Customs.

c)   Disclose certain **illegal activities** to appropriate public authorities. Not all illegal activities (whether by clients, employers or colleagues) must be reported in this way: there may be other regulatory machinery for dealing with them (as we will see in chapter 4). However, some activities are covered by specific legal provisions, particularly in relation to public safety, organised crime and terrorism.

HOW IT WORKS

Your in-tray this morning contains several requests for information.

- An estate agent has written to request a financial reference (confirmation of income etc) for one of your clients who has applied to rent a property.

  You phone the client to ask her permission to give this information to the estate agent (confirming the details of his identity). You ask her to confirm her authorisation by e-mail.

  You send the information addressed to the estate agent by name, clearly marked 'private and confidential'.

- You receive a formal demand from HM Revenue and Customs (citing its statutory powers under the VAT Act 1994) for information regarding the VAT returns of a client.

  You report this to Sheila, who says she will refer the matter to the firm's legal advisers.

- A property developer, who is a client of yours, has written asking whether you know of any businesses in the city looking to sell a commercial property.

  You recall that your petrol station clients had told you that they were intending to sell. However, you are also aware that the value of the property (for its current purposes) will fall once the by-pass scheme is announced. Both these facts are covered by client confidentiality.

  You call the petrol station owners and ask them if you can disclose their plans to the property developer. They give permission, so you pass the message to the developer. At the same time, you advise him of the need to carry out 'due diligence' for any purchase, including checking any development applications already under consideration by the Town Planners – without suggesting any specific reason to do so. You follow up with a letter to both the petrol station owners and the property developers, recommending that they seek independent advice regarding the sale/purchase: this enables you to avoid taking on a conflict of interest between the two clients (if one wins and one loses from the transaction).

- The new receptionist has given you her banking details, for payroll. She has also included some information about the rates of pay and benefits paid by her previous employer, and some of its payroll practices – apparently just to explain how delighted she is by the generosity and integrity of Belgiorno Bellman.

    This data may have been given in good faith – but it is inappropriate to disclose confidential details of a previous employer. You delete the email, having recorded the relevant banking details. You also make a note to have a quiet word with the receptionist about confidentiality.

student notes ✎

Signpost

See the *AAT Ethical Guidelines*:

- **Section 140**: Confidentiality

Money laundering

A key example of the mandatory disclosure of illegal activities is the case of **money laundering**. MONEY LAUNDERING is a process by which criminals attempt to conceal the true origin and ownership of the proceeds of their criminal activity. In UK law, it is an offence to obtain, conceal or invest funds or property, if you know or suspect that they are the proceeds of criminal conduct or terrorist funding ('criminal property').

You may think that you are unlikely to come across criminal property – but it isn't all about the kinds of crime you see on TV cop shows! It includes the proceeds of tax evasion, benefits obtained through bribery and corruption, and benefits (eg saved costs) arising from a failure to comply with a regulatory requirement (eg cutting corners on health and safety provisions).

Financial institutions and non-financial businesses and professions are required to adopt specific measures to help identify and prevent money laundering and terrorist financing, including:

- Implementing client checking, record-keeping and internal suspicion-reporting measures. This includes the appointment of a Money Laundering Reporting Officer.

- Not doing or disclosing anything that might prejudice an investigation into such activities. This specifically includes any word or action that might 'tip off' the money launderers that they are, or may come, under investigation. (You are, however, entitled to advise clients on issues regarding prevention of money laundering, say, on a non-specific basis.)

- Disclosing any knowledge or suspicion of money laundering activity to the appropriate authorities. It is specifically stated that accounting professionals will not be in breach of their professional duty of confidence (and therefore cannot be sued) if they report, in good faith, any knowledge or suspicions in relation to money laundering, to the appropriate authority.

Statutes	<ul><li>Criminal Justice Act 1993</li><li>Terrorism Act 2000</li><li>Proceeds of Crime Act 2002</li><li>Money Laundering Regulations 2003</li><li>Money Laundering Regulations 2007</li></ul>(So you can see what a Hot Topic this is!)
What should be reported	Any knowledge or suspicion that you may be in danger of assisting a money launderer in possessing, using or concealing the proceeds of crime.(Note, however, that you need to have reasonable grounds for your suspicions. Disclosure without such grounds lays you open to being sued for breach of confidentiality.)
To whom	<ul><li>The Money Laundering Reporting Officer in your firm (where applicable)</li><li>Serious Organised Crime Agency (SOCA)</li></ul>

Signpost

The AAT has issued separate guidance on money laundering, available from its website: www.aat.org.uk. This is likely to be too detailed for Unit 32 assessment purposes, but you should be aware that detailed guidance exists, if you encounter a situation in which you think it might be relevant.

HOW IT WORKS

You are still a bit worried about your café client. When you visited the café recently, you noticed that they had employed an additional chef – but now, checking the payroll reports, you can't find any mention of this person, or any payments made to her.

You need to check that your suspicions (that the employee is being paid cash to avoid tax liabilities) are well-founded, but you are aware of the danger of 'tipping off' the client. Payroll fraud is an offence, reportable to the SOCA (or Money Laundering Reporting Officer in your firm): if you prepare financial statements covering it up, you are party to the concealment of 'criminal property'.

Your first step is to discuss the matter with Sheila. She advises you to speak to the clients in general terms about the seriousness of accurate and truthful reporting. If the situation doesn't then change (and the payroll 'omission' isn't put right), Belgiorno Bellman's MLRO will be consulted.

You are reminded of this discussion later in the day, when you go to the local Discount Electrical store to buy a new television. You hesitate over the prices, and the salesman offers you a great deal – if you pay cash, 'no questions asked'. The store isn't a client, and the matter hasn't arisen in the course of your professional work – so you have no reporting responsibility. However, since you want to preserve your personal integrity (as an Accounting Technician), you refuse the offer and decide to shop elsewhere for your new TV.

Factors to consider in disclosing information

Even if the information can legitimately be disclosed, you still have to consider a number of points in deciding whether or how to proceed.

- **How reliable is the information?** If all the relevant facts are known and supported by good evidence, the disclosure may be clear cut – but if all you have is unsupported facts, opinions or suspicions, you may have to use your professional judgement as to whether you disclose, how and to whom.

- **Who is the appropriate recipient of the information?** You need to be sure that the person to whom you give the information is the right person: in other words, (s)he has a legitimate right to it, and the authority to act on it.

- **Will you incur legal liability by disclosing the information?** Some disclosures (such as reporting money laundering) are legally 'privileged': you cannot be sued for breach of professional confidentiality – as long as the disclosure is made in good faith and with reasonable grounds. Other situations may not be so clear cut, however: you may need to consider getting advice from a solicitor before proceeding with a disclosure without the client's authorisation.

- **How can you protect the on-going confidentiality of the information as far as possible?** If you make a disclosure, you have a responsibility to ensure that it is made only to the relevant parties, and that they understand their responsibilities to protect the information from further disclosure. At least, ensure that you send the information direct to the relevant party, clearly labelled 'confidential' or 'for your eyes only'.

Activity 6

Your friend has been offered a lucrative supply contract by a large company, which is a client of your firm. Having prepared its accounts, you are aware that the company is in serious financial difficulties – to the point that it may not be able to meet its financial obligations to your friend.

What can you disclose, to whom and how?

CONTRACTUAL OBLIGATIONS

You have a legal obligation to fulfil the terms of a **contract for services** (to clients) and/or a **contract of service** (to your employer).

A CONTRACT is an agreement which legally binds the parties to it, to fulfil the terms of the agreement on both sides. If the terms are not fulfilled on either side, the party failing to do this is 'in breach of contract' – with potentially serious legal consequences.

A **contract to provide professional services** to a client (usually set out in a letter of engagement) should contain specific terms – to which both parties agree – in regard to:

a)   what must be done (duties and responsibilities)
b)   by whom
c)   for whom
d)   by when
e)   in return for what fees or remuneration
f)   with what obligation of due care and
g)   with what ownership rights in documents and records

in order for the contract to be considered as 'performed' or 'discharged': in other words, successfully completed.

A **contract of service** or employment will similarly contain specific terms, in regard to the employees' duties, responsibilities and entitlements (to specific remuneration, conditions of work, holidays and so on).

However, in addition to specifically-included or **express** terms, there will also be **implied** terms: obligations and entitlements which can, in a sense, be taken for granted because they are already covered by the law and/or accepted practice. (So, for example, a client contract need not state that information will be confidential, and an employment contract need not state that the employer will provide a healthy and safe working environment: these obligations are understood.)

It is also worth remembering that a contract does not have to be in writing. A **verbal agreement** can make a valid (and enforceable) contract, as long as there is some form of offer and acceptance (mutual agreement), consideration (mutual exchange of benefits) and intention to create legal relations (mutual understanding that the agreement will be legally binding). As a point of general integrity, if you say you'll do something – do it!

We will look in more detail at contracts of employment in chapter 4, and contracts for services in chapter 5.

We will now go on to look at the application of some of the principles discussed so far, in particular professional work situations.

PREPARING FINANCIAL STATEMENTS

A key part of professional and technical competence is to present financial information fully, honestly and clearly (so that it can be understood in its context). As we saw earlier, this is also a key element in preventing or avoiding fraud.

Financial information should:

- Clearly describe the true nature of transactions, assets and liabilities, building up an accurate picture of the business's financial position

- Be prepared and presented in accordance with accepted accounting standards, classifying and recording entries in a timely and proper manner (as covered in your earlier studies).

Activity 7

Give three examples of dishonest or misleading use or presentation of financial information.

Signpost

See the *AAT Ethical Guidelines*:

- **Section 320**: Preparation and reporting of information

TAXATION SERVICES

Particular ethical issues are raised by performing taxation services (preparing tax returns, giving tax advice and so on), since there is a complex administrative and legal framework for both direct taxation (based on income, gains, profits and losses) and indirect taxation (such as Value Added Tax).

The AAT's Sponsoring Bodies which deal with taxation, and the Chartered Institute of Taxation, have extensive ethical guidelines in this area – and the AAT's own guidelines recommend that UK members seek advice from the Director of Professional Development where required.

Key issues are **integrity**, **technical competence** and **confidentiality**. The following general principles, covered in the Guidelines, apply to both direct and indirect taxation.

Managing expectations and communications

- When you submit a tax return or computations for a client or employer, you are acting as an **agent** of the taxpayer. This requires a clear understanding, on both sides, of the nature and scope of your duties. For a client, these are set out in the terms of an 'engagement letter' (as discussed in chapter 5).

- Employers or clients may form fixed expectations of the outcome of your advice or services. You need to ensure that they understand that you are only able to offer **opinions** – not promises: tax returns and advice are always open to challenge.

- If your advice or opinion is likely to have a significant effect, you should **record** it (in a letter or memorandum, kept in your files), for clarity – and letter evidence, if required.

- If you are acting (as a member in practice) for a client, you should supply him or her with **copies** of all tax computations before you submit them to the Revenue office.

Activity 8

What should you do if a client asks you how much tax you will be able to save them this year?

Ethical reporting

- You have a duty to **put forward the best position**, in favour of your employer or client. However, you need to ensure that you do this with **integrity** (not falsifying the position), **objectivity** (on the basis of the facts), **professional competence** (in line with technical standards and procedures) and **compliance** (in line with the law).

- You have a duty towards the tax authorities to **provide information in good faith**. You should only undertake tax work on the understanding that your client or employer will make **full and accurate disclosure** of the relevant information. While you need to exercise reasonable care in accepting and presenting information on their behalf, it is the taxpayer (the client or employer) who bears ultimate responsibility for the accuracy of the data and computations: don't take on responsibility for the accuracy or completeness of information which is outside your own knowledge.

■ Do not associate yourself with a tax return or related communication if you have any reason to believe that it is **false** or **misleading**.

– If it contains a false or misleading statement

– If it leaves out or obscures information which should be submitted, in such a way as to mislead the tax authorities

– If it contains statements or information which have been provided carelessly, without the taxpayer checking or knowing whether they are true or false (and therefore being potentially false or misleading)

What if you become aware of errors or omissions?

■ If you become aware of a significant error or omission in a tax return from a previous year, or of a failure to file a required tax return, you must immediately advise your client or employer – and recommend that they inform the Revenue office. (It is not normally your duty to make the disclosure, and you shouldn't do so without the permission of the client or employer, as a confidentiality issue.)

■ If an employer or client refuses to correct the problem, you should inform them that you cannot act for them in regard to that return or communication. If you are a self-employed practitioner, you should cease to act for the client, and inform them in writing. You should also inform the Revenue that you have ceased to act for that client – adding (where relevant, and only if you yourself were acting for the client in regard to the error or omission) that you have received information indicating that the accounts or statements should not be relied upon.

The HM Revenue and Customs authorities have extensive legal powers (under the Taxes Management Act and VAT Act) to obtain information that may otherwise be withheld. If a statutory demand for information is made, you should seek legal advice.

You should also note that for the purposes of money laundering provisions, the proceeds of deliberate tax evasion – including under-declaring income and over-claiming expenses – are just as much 'criminal property' as money from drug trafficking, terrorist activity or theft! You therefore have a duty to report the client or employer's activities to the authority, as discussed earlier.

student notes

Activity 9

What should you do if you become aware of a significant error in a tax return which you prepared and submitted for a client in a previous year?

HOW IT WORKS

You have been thinking over your misgivings about the café client. While you were able to ensure that personal expenditures were not, after all, reflect in the accounts of the business, you haven't had a satisfactory response in regard to the undeclared income from the office catering service.

The owners supplied you with a general assurance, in writing, that all income was being declared. However, you have lingering doubts. The business does not seem to be reducing its purchases of supplies, nor the hours of its delivery staff – yet recorded sales are still very low, especially compared to comparable periods in previous years. At the same time, you note that mobile phone costs of all staff are being claimed as business expenses on the grounds of 'extensive off-site trading'.

It is now time to prepare the café's tax return.

Having discussed the matter with Sheila, you meet with the client to ensure that they understand that they are responsible for making full and accurate disclosure to the tax authorities, and are prepared to sign a statement to this effect. They reply that, as they see it, you are supposed to be 'on their side' to save them tax. You explain your professional and legal obligations and emphasise that you cannot knowingly associate yourself with a misleading return. As long as you have reason to believe that there may be errors or omissions, you will not be able to act for the café in preparing or submitting this return.

Signpost

See the *AAT Ethical Guidelines*:

- **Section 160**: Taxation services

INTERNAL AUDIT

Internal audit is part of the internal control system of an organisation, designed to examine and evaluate the adequacy and effectiveness of other controls.

When providing internal audit services, the key ethical issue is **independence**. Independence is a fundamental concept of auditing – and this applies just as much to the internal auditor as to the external auditor.

How can internal auditors be 'independent' in their relationship with an organisation, though, since it employs them and pays their wages – and the people being audited are their colleagues?

- Although an internal audit department is part of an organisation, it should be independent of the line management whose sphere of authority it may audit – otherwise the findings may be biased or influenced.

- Internal auditors should not install new procedures or systems, nor engage in the activities which are being appraised – as this might also compromise their independence.

- There should be a clear responsibility structure. The internal audit department must have direct reporting access to senior management and independent arbiters (such as an audit committee) if relevant.

- The auditor's own approach should be highly professional, objective, detached and honest. Each individual should consider matters such as:

  - avoiding conflicts of interest

  - freedom from undue influences and pressures within the organisation

  - retaining objectivity when auditing areas he has responsibility for.

CHAPTER OVERVIEW

■ In a corporate context, fraud can fall into two main categories:

  – Removal of funds or assets from a business

  – Intentional misrepresentation of the financial position of the business

■ Fraud is a serious matter, in that it has potentially significant negative impacts on organisations and their members. It also has legal consequences.

■ The integrity of professional services is protected by:

  – Independence of mind: objectivity, free of bias, prejudice or partiality

  – Independence in appearance: being 'beyond reproach', so that a reasonable and informed observer would find no cause to think that objectivity was threatened.

■ General safeguards to objectivity and independence include strength of character, professionalism, and legal and professional accountability.

■ One clear threat to perceived objectivity is soliciting or accepting significant gifts, services, favours or hospitality from parties who may be seeking to influence the outcome. (This is also illegal for employees of public bodies, under anti-corruption legislation.)

■ Accountants have a duty of confidentiality to clients, not to use or disclose information obtained in the course of professional work, unless:

  – They are properly authorised to do so
  – They have a professional duty to do so
  – They have a legal duty to do so (eg in the case of suspicion of money laundering)

■ Where there is a contract for services (to clients) or a contract for service (to an employer), the accountant has a duty to comply with both express and implied terms.

■ Particular obligations apply in regard to preparing financial statements, providing taxation services and providing internal audit services.

> **KEY WORDS**
>
> **Fraud** is deception by deceit.
>
> **Stakeholders** are groups which have a legitimate interest (or stake) in a business and its performance. This wil include owners, employees and creditors.
>
> **Money laundering** is the concealment of the origin and ownership of the proceeds of crime.
>
> A **contract** is an agreement which legally binds the parties to it to fulfil its terms.

HOW MUCH HAVE YOU LEARNED?

1   List six examples of fraud based on the removal of funds or assets from a business.

2   How can year-end cut-off dates be manipulated to perpetrate fraud?

3   Give three examples of stakeholders in a business, who may suffer as the result of fraudulent activity.

4   If you are acting as an agent for a client, and a third party offers you a gift which might be seen to influence your actions in relation to your principal's business, is this illegal, or just unethical?

5   Give three examples of types of information which would be regarded as confidential.

6   You read with interest an article in a small business magazine, which appears to have been written by a client of yours, a VAT-registered sole trader.

You look up the on-line archive of the magazine and find that your client has supplied a number of articles over the last two years – and is billed as a 'well-known writer on the subject'. The web site also indicates that generous fees are offered by publishers for such technical articles. The client's accounts, however, show no income from this source: neither this year, nor last year (when the client engaged another firm of accountants to prepare his tax return).

What ethical issue arises from this – and what should you do?

7   Six months ago, you were transferred from the payroll department (where you were employed for three years) to the firm's internal audit department. You have now been asked to review and report on the internal controls operating in the HR systems of the firm, including recruitment/selection, training and payroll.

What ethical issue arises from this – and what should you do?

chapter 3:
PERSONAL AND INTERPERSONAL SKILLS

INTERPERSONAL SKILLS FOR ETHICAL INTERACTIONS

INTERPERSONAL SKILLS are skills that are used in interactions between (inter-) people: communication, influencing and persuasion, negotiation, assertiveness and so on.

Interpersonal skills are about managing relationships and interactions with other people. So how does this relate to professional ethics?

- **We should treat other people in ethical ways:** fairly, respectfully and appropriately. There are many professional situations in which we need to influence people, for example – but there are ethical ways of doing this (by argument and persuasion) and unethical ways of doing it (by deception, manipulation or coercion). One way of putting it is that we need to value people and use objects: not the other way around!

- **We may need to manage ethical issues in co-operation or conflict with other people.** As we saw in chapter 1, there may be honest differences of opinion about ethical matters – and we need to ensure that these do not become barriers to our working relationships. We may need to teach and persuade others to behave more ethically. And we may need to discuss, negotiate and resolve ethical conflicts.

Communication

COMMUNICATION is the key to good working relationships with colleagues, superiors and subordinates, clients – and just about anyone we come into contact with!

Communication is about putting across your message as clearly as possible (bearing in mind the needs and abilities of your audience) and checking that your message has been understood in the way you intended.

Professional and ethical communication means:

- Honesty, openness and clarity in giving information. (Particularly when advising clients or colleagues who are not technical experts – or when dealing with someone whose first language is not English: be careful not to abuse your power in the situation…)

- Respecting the confidentiality of personal and financial information.

- Communicating in ways that respect the other person's rights as well as your own: this is sometimes called **assertive communication**, which we discuss further below. You are entitled to state your own opinions, feelings and needs – but it is only fair to allow others to do the same.

■ Avoiding discriminatory or derogatory language. This is a matter of law in the UK – but you should strive for courtesy and respect in any case: they are an important part of appropriate professional behaviour.

■ Observing appropriate conventions, formats and guidelines for communication in your profession and organisation. Examples include the style of letter-writing or report-writing; policies on the use of e-mail; courteous telephone technique and so on.

Activity 1

What particular communication issues might arise if you needed to:

a) explain capital gains tax to a self-employed female painter/decorator whose first language is not English?

b) resolve a grievance you have against a colleague in the Accounts section, who is constantly criticising your work to others?

HOW IT WORKS

Choice of communication method

There is a wide variety of possible communication methods for any given task. You have to choose which is the most appropriate for the circumstances and for the message you want to convey.

Face to face verbal communication is frequently the most effective, as you can express yourself fully and gain immediate feedback. However, this may not be possible, due to time constraints or physical location. For complex subjects, or matters with legal implications, it may also be better to communicate in **writing**, so that the recipient can consider the details – and refer back to them when required. (This is often the case in dealing with ethical questions.) A written document also provides a record of the issues considered.

Styles of communication

In order to be effective in achieving your aims from an interpersonal encounter, you need to adopt the right style or approach.

Depending on the nature of the interaction, and the relationship between the parties, this may be **formal** or **informal**. In your professional role, you may choose to be on the formal side – until you have 'permission' (based on the other person's behaviour towards you) to adopt a more informal style.

Your style should also reflect your purpose in communicating.

Informing. The most important questions are: who are you talking to, what do they already know – and what do they need to know? Keep information as clear, simple and precise as possible, and avoid technical jargon which non-experts will not understand.

Influencing. If you are trying to influence or persuade someone (eg if you need to persuade your employer or client to alter unethical practices), you need to communicate clearly and assertively, and give the other people a good reason to come round to your way of thinking: for example persuasive arguments or benefits for them.

Questioning. If you are seeking information, it helps to be clear about exactly what you need to know. However, you also need to listen actively and keep your mind open, in order to receive the answers.

Requesting help. If you are asking someone to do something for you, 'begging' isn't an assertive approach. Stating clearly what you need – and how helping you will benefit the other person (or team) – is likely to be more effective.

Resolving conflict. Again, a clear and honest statement of the problem (as you see it, without blaming the other person) is an assertive start. Conflict is a two-way process, so conflict resolution also requires give-and-take: active listening, collaborative problem-solving and willingness to negotiate (if possible).

HOW IT WORKS

It is 5 o'clock on a Thursday evening, and one of the senior partners approaches your desk. 'Good, you're still here,' he says. 'We've got a group of trainees starting tomorrow, and I wanted to give them a presentation on professional ethics. George was going to do it – but he's been called away to a conference all week. You're not doing anything this evening, are you?'

Your first tasks in relation to this incident will be communication tasks!

- You decide that rather than giving in ('Well, I was busy, but... I suppose I could...') or losing your temper, you will give an assertive response (bearing in mind the senior partner's status). You are, in fact, busy this evening: you say so, calmly and clearly. You tell him that, in any case, you will need to consult with Sheila, since you have prior commitments to her and to your clients. You suggest (being firm, but co-operative) that if the presentation could be held over until Monday, you would be willing to work on it over the weekend. The senior partner agrees to this.

- You e-mail Sheila, to inform her of the request, and ask her to let you know as soon as possible if she has any problem with your taking the time on Monday. She replies that it will be a good experience for you – and suggests that you ask a junior accounting technician, Bob, to take over your routine tasks on Monday.

- On Friday morning, you speak to Bob personally. You are friendly and persuasive, emphasising how much you would appreciate his help. You stress that the tasks shouldn't be too time-consuming, but will be good learning experience for Bob. He agrees. You follow-up later with an e-mail thanking him, and arranging to meet on Monday to talk through the tasks.

- You also e-mail George, informing him that you have been asked to 'take over' his presentation. You ask if he has any preparatory notes or slides already prepared, and whether he would mind your using them.

Good work: you have proactively taken steps to defuse potential strains on each of these relationships, by thoughtful communication.

You may have covered the commonly-used formats and styles of business communication in your studies for Unit 31: Accounting Work Skills. Here, we will briefly review some of the skills specifically mentioned in the range statement for Element 32.1: letter and report writing, and discussion and negotiation.

LETTERS

Letters can be used for a wide variety of communication tasks, including: creating a formal relationship with clients (a letter of engagement); giving or requesting information; drawing attention to information supplied (a covering letter); or communicating in formal or personal situations with employers (eg a formal letter of protest or resignation).

Modern business letters contain some standard elements:

Letterhead

'Private and confidential' (if applicable)

Recipient's name and address

Date

Dear Sir/Dear Ms Brown

Subject heading

Main body of the letter (introduction; clear paragraphs of content; conclusion)

Yours faithfully/ Yours sincerely

Author's signature
Author's name and position

'Enc.' (if something is enclosed with the letter) or
'Cc.' (if a copy of the letter has been sent to someone else)

Activity 2

a)   If you start a letter 'Dear Ms Rofakalu', how should you sign off?
b)   How should you address a letter to a firm?
c)   Why is it important to include a 'cc' or copy reference?
d)   What kind of things might be enclosed with a covering letter?

The key points of business-like letter-writing style are as follows.

- ■   Beginning. The reader will not be as familiar with the context of the message as you are! Explain briefly why you are writing. ('Thank you for your letter of 3 March, in which you requested information about auditing services.' Or 'I have been asked by my colleague,

George Brown, to contact you with regard to your enquiry about auditing services.')

- Middle. The middle paragraph(s) should contain the substance of your response to a previous message, or details of the matter in hand, or the information you wish to communicate. If you are making several points, start a new paragraph with each, so the reader can digest them more easily.

- End. Summarise your main point briefly, or make clear exactly what response is required of the reader. ('I look forward to meeting you to discuss the matter in more detail', or 'If you require any further information, please call me'.)

HOW IT WORKS

So, it's still Friday at Belgiorno Bellman. Your 'To Do' list for the day includes the following.

- Draft formal letter of engagement to Marchand & Sons: re engagement to provide financial management consultancy (Use specimen format)

- Covering letter for draft funding proposal for JBL Ltd: draw attention to key points of proposal and request amendments ASAP.

- Reply to enquiry letter re fees and charges

- Letter to café client, formally ceasing to act for them (get Sheila to check: copy to legal department)

- Letter of complaint to Telecom, re faulty equipment supplied last week

- Note of thanks to Jim for introducing new client

See how widely used letters are!

REPORTS

You may be required to use a variety of reports in the course of your work, from short informal reports (which may be included in a letter, memo or e-mail), to highly-structured formal reports and financial reports (which have their own specific conventions and requirements).

The main points when writing formal reports are that:

- The **style** should be business-like, concise and impersonal. Avoid the kind of expressions and contractions that you might associate with speech between friends: you might say 'I couldn't see what the fuss was about', but in a formal report you would write 'I was unable to identify the cause of the conflict' or even 'The cause of the conflict was not apparent' (dropping the personal 'I' altogether).

- The **argument** should be balanced. Give both sides of the story, before reaching a conclusion. Give evidence or support for any opinion or recommendation you put forward. If you have lots of supporting details or statistics, consider putting them in a separate numbered appendix (clearly referred to in the text).

- The **structure** should be clear and logical. Certain standard headings may be used (see below) to divide the content up systematically for the reader. Under each heading, your text should be further broken up into short topic paragraphs, so that it is easy to read and follow.

REPORT HEADING

Private and confidential (if relevant)

Prepared by:
Prepared for:
Date:
Subject:

EXECUTIVE SUMMARY		[If the report is very long, to give a quick overview]
I	INTRODUCTION	[Or Background; or Situation]
II	FINDINGS	[Or Analysis; or appropriate topic heading(s)]
III	CONCLUSION	[Or Summary; or Recommendations, if asked for]
APPENDICES		[If any]

HOW IT WORKS

Also on your To Do list, for the coming week at Belgiorno Bellman, are the following tasks.

- Report for senior partners on 'Issues in Client Identification and Appraisal, in light of the Money Laundering Regulations 2003' (see Seminar notes)

- Report (commissioned by Barnt Green Electrical) on fraud prevention measures

- Report for Sheila on my CPD plans for next 12 months (Personal Development Plan)

- Note-form report to Sheila tracing history of action taken re café client

DISCUSSION AND NEGOTIATION

Discussion and negotiation are **face to face** communication media, and as such are rather more complicated than written media (where you get to prepare and check your messages before sending them). They are highly interactive, allowing questions and responses in real time. They also involve various forms of non-verbal communication (personal appearance, body language and tone of voice), so they provide much more information than written or even telephone conversations.

This makes them particularly useful for argument, persuasion, conflict resolution and the handling of personally 'sensitive' matters. Which makes them particularly useful for raising and resolving ethical issues!

Constructive discussion

Some principles of constructive discussion include the following.

- **Establish safe conditions.** If the discussion is likely to be sensitive, it should be private, uninterrupted and confidential (as understood by both parties). The nature and topic of the discussion needs to be clearly identified at the start, to give both parties time to get their thoughts in order. (You don't persuade someone by 'mugging' them with ideas!)

- **Balance speaking with listening.** Discussion is 'dialogue', not 'monologue': two-way, not one-way. Set up ground rules, if necessary, for each party to listen (without interrupting), show that they have understood what the other person has just said (by summarising) and then respond, in turn.

- **Listen actively.** Purposely try to understand what the other person is trying to say. Be attentive and encouraging (eg by nodding or saying 'uh huh' occasionally!) Ask questions. Summarise key points.

- **Communicate clearly.** Be brief and straightforward. Use language that you think the other person will understand (watching out for technical jargon). Check from time to time that the other person is getting the message (eg by looking out for a perplexed expression, or saying 'Does that make sense to you?').

- **Manage your emotions.** Strong emotions such as nervousness, anger and frustration get in the way of listening and clear communication. If a discussion 'triggers' emotion in you, take a moment to breath deeply and calm yourself.

- **Control your body language.** Fidgeting, avoiding eye contact or waving your arms gives out messages – which may not be the ones you want to convey! (Calm, confident body language can even help you feel calm and confident...)

- **Acknowledge where the other person has a point.** Focus on 'common ground' (things you can both agree on) where possible: they may give you a way of moving the discussion forward in a co-operative way.

- **Agree to disagree, where necessary.** You don't have to 'win' every ethical argument: only those which compromise your own professional standards.

Activity 3

What are the advantages and disadvantages of face to face discussion for:

a) challenging a colleague or client whom you suspect of dishonest behaviour?

b) agreeing your contractual obligations to an employer or client?

Assertive communication

ASSERTIVENESS involves standing up for your own rights – but in such a way that you do not violate another person's rights: expressing your needs, wants, opinions, feelings and beliefs in direct and honest (but appropriate) ways.

This is clearly not the same as 'passive' behaviour (where you give way to the wishes and beliefs of others) – but it is also not the same as 'aggressive' behaviour (where you ignore or steamroll over the needs, feelings or opinions of others).

Examples of assertive behaviour in an ethical disagreement or conflict may be:

- Stating clearly, calmly and objectively if you think an instruction or action is unethical – without blaming, accusing or insulting the other person.

- Using specific statements instead of generalisations or exaggerations, especially when disagreeing or giving criticism.

- Sticking to your own beliefs, when necessary, without getting angry, defensive or apologetic.

Negotiating solutions

NEGOTIATION isn't just about forcing someone's price down – or your fee or salary up! It is a style of communication, which can be used to reach agreements and solve problems in all kinds of areas – including ethical conflicts.

Negotiation is a problem-solving technique. The objective is for both parties to reach **agreement**, so that they both go away with a decision they can live with – without damaging the **relationship** between them.

This is a process of:

- **Purposeful persuasion** (where each party attempts to persuade the other to accept its case, by using clear, logical arguments).

- **Constructive compromise** (where each party accepts that they may need to meet the other party half way, so that both parties 'win' something – if not everything they originally wanted).

Activity 4

What kinds of negotiation might you expect to take part in as part of your work role?

An informal negotiation will look a lot like the kind of constructive discussion we outlined earlier. A basic 'win-win' approach to negotiating may be as follows.

Step 1   Map out what the needs and fears of both parties are: why might each party be taking the position they are taking?

Step 2   Define your own desired outcome from the negotiation and estimate the worst, realistic and best case scenarios. (What is the best you can expect – and what is the least you will settle for? What might be an acceptable compromise?)

Step 3   Look for mutual or trade-off benefits. How might your solution offer benefits to the other party as well? What might be a cheap concession for you to give, that would be valuable for the other party to receive (if it came down to straight bargaining)?

Step 4   Spell out the positive benefits of your position to the other party. Make it as easy as possible for them to agree with you! Emphasise areas of agreement and common ground. Overcome negativity and opposition by asking questions such as: 'What would it take to make this work for you?' or 'How is this going to get us where we need to go?'

Step 5   Be flexible and ready to compromise or make trade-offs if necessary.

Step 6   Be hard on the issue, but soft on the person. If you are dealing with a client, employer or colleague, 'winning' isn't the objective: you are trying to co-operate in solving a problem that affects you both.

Step 7   Take notes, so the accuracy of everyone's recollection of what was proposed and agreed can be checked.

Step 8   Summarise and confirm the details of your agreement to both parties (eg by letter, memo or e-mail). And describe it, as far as possible, as a mutually positive outcome!

Activity 5

Your employer instructs you to 'lose' some invoices which raise discrepancies in the company's accounts. You state clearly that you are not able to do this, as it would breach your professional standards – both technical and ethical. Later in the day, you sit down to discuss (or negotiate) the matter.

a)   What best, worst and 'fall back' options will you go into the discussion with?

b)   Give an example of how this discussion might end in a:

-    win-win outcome (where both parties benefit)

-    win-lose outcome (where one party benefits at the other's expense)

-    lose-lose outcome (where neither party benefits)

c)   What communication techniques and approaches will be most useful to you in this encounter?

CONTINUING PROFESSIONAL DEVELOPMENT (CPD)

We turn now from interpersonal skills to a cluster of extremely important personal skills: flexibility, self-development and continuous learning!

Continuing Professional Development (CPD) has a crucial role in ensuring that you maintain your **technical** and **professional competence**, keeping pace with changes in your work role and the practices, techniques and standards of your profession.

The AAT Council has recommended a programme of a minimum of 30 hours' CPD each year for members.

How do you know when you need more learning?

Some training needs will emerge in the course of your work. If your organisation introduces new equipment or software, you may need to learn how to use it! You may also identify your own shortcomings (missed deadlines, subjects on which you had to get help from others, times when you didn't get the results you wanted) as learning opportunities.

Training needs may also be identified for you, as you get informal performance feedback from your supervisors and colleagues – or through formal appraisal interviews.

Other training needs may be identified as you keep in touch with developments in your professional environment: through the Internet, professional journals (such as Accounting Technician), and networking opportunities through your professional body.

HOW IT WORKS

- Chatting in the kitchen with the firm's legal adviser, you hear about forthcoming legislation which will redefine 'corruption' and harmonise EU anti-corruption law. You make a note to look this up on the Internet, and to look out for briefings in the professional journals.

- Browsing through the financial press, you read about a newly-published IFRS. You make a note to see if the firm's library has a copy.

- On the office noticeboard, someone has posted an advertisement for a seminar on the use of the latest software tools for financial managers: this interests you, because you have never seen some of them demonstrated properly.

- Sheila has just returned from a conference on CPD, and offers to give you some coaching and mentoring, where 'areas for improvement' have been identified in your annual performance appraisal.

- You have asked the tax manager to check your calculations for a client, since they involve aspects of the tax regime that you don't know well. She comes back to you with your calculations covered in corrections and amendments. 'We're getting more and more clients in the same position', says the tax manager. 'You'll need to get a better grip on the technicalities than this!'

Learning resources and opportunities for CPD

There is a huge menu of learning resources and opportunities available, including:

- Courses, workshops and information seminars

- Books, quality newspapers, professional journals and technical publications (such as accounting standards, legislation and court reports)

- Videos, CD-ROM and computer software packages for education and training

- Web sites (for obtaining information and accessing training and materials)

- Instruction and procedure manuals used in your organisation (eg to teach you to use equipment and software, or comply with organisational procedures and practices)

And there are two other very valuable sources of learning which are often neglected.

- **Other people**

  Your superiors and colleagues at work are an excellent potential source of information, advice and instruction/coaching in areas where they are more expert or experienced than you are. They may be able to help you access opportunities (eg nominating you for training programmes or secondments). They are also in a great position to offer you feedback (about your strengths and weaknesses, learning/improvement needs and how you are doing in your learning).

  Professional networks provide similar support and guidance within your wider professional sphere.

- **Your own experience**

  'Doing something' is an important development technique! Identify opportunities to try a new technique or approach at work, which you could use as a learning opportunity. If you want to learn to contribute more effectively to meetings, for example, what meetings could you arrange to participate in and observe? Whom could you ask for feedback?

Activity 6

You have made a note in your CPD journal that your knowledge of health and safety law has become outdated by the vast amounts of legislation arising from European Directives in recent years.

a) How important is this for you?
b) What (if anything) could you do to update your knowledge?

CHAPTER OVERVIEW

- Interpersonal skills are important in managing relationships and interactions in ethical ways. They also help us to manage ethical issues and conflicts effectively.

- Ethical communication involves honesty and clarity in giving information; respecting confidentiality; being appropriately assertive; and observing professional guidelines and formats.

- Letter writing and report writing are key business communication skills.

> **KEY WORDS**
>
> **Interpersonal skills** are used in interactions between people.
>
> **Assertiveness** is clear, honest communication based on protecting your rights without violating the rights of others.
>
> **Negotiation** is a process of purposeful persuasion and constructive compromise with a view to reaching agreement.

- Face to face discussions are particularly effective for argument, persuasion, conflict resolution and negotiation, because of their interactive nature and potential for non-verbal (as well as verbal) communication.

- Both constructive discussion and negotiation require two-way dialogue, involving active listening and collaborative problem-solving, aiming for a 'win-win' outcome where possible.

- Continuing Professional Development activities ensure that you maintain your technical and professional competence, keeping pace with changes in your work role and the practices, techniques and standards of your profession.

- CPD involves both formal and informal learning experiences.

HOW MUCH HAVE YOU LEARNED?

1   What is 'active listening'?

2   Distinguish between an ethical and an unethical approach to influencing other people.

3   You are employed in the internal audit department of a large firm. One of the line managers, whose department you are currently reviewing, takes you aside privately one morning and asks you how the work is going. You say that it's going well – but that, of course, you can't discuss the details until you make your report. The manager grows insistent, telling you that 'for the sake of fairness' you really ought to give him warning of any adverse findings, so that he has a chance to put things right. 'You know how tough things are at the moment,' he says. 'You wouldn't want to get your colleagues in trouble, would you? Just give me an idea: call it "constructive feedback". I promise, we'll put things right – and no-one else will know. You'll have done us all a favour.'

a)   What are the ethical issues here?

b)   Give an example of an assertive response to the manager's request.

4   You are employed as an accounting technician in a firm of chartered accountants. You have just received the following letter.

X L Financial Services
93 Hammond Terrace
Guildford
Surrey GU2 5LP

Jafford Jolley (Chartered Accountants)
3 Southford Square
London SE 3 2BX

13 May 200X

Dear Sirs

Transatlantic Trading Limited

We have recently been engaged to provide investment advice to the above client.

With the client's authorisation, we respectfully request that you provide us with all financial records, books and statements prepared by you on behalf of the above client, at your earliest convenience.

Yours faithfully

G J Gillespie
Consultant

You have not, as far as you know, had any communication from Transatlantic Trading Limited on this matter.

a)   Draft an e-mail to your supervisor James Benedetti, checking whatever information you require to take further action.

b)   Assuming that James has also had no communication from Transatlantic Trading Limited, draft a letter to G J Gillespie.

5   You are employed in the Accounts Department of a large manufacturing firm. Under a new mentoring-type scheme, you and another Accounting Technician (who has just started at the firm) have been assigned to each other as 'Development Buddies': your aim is to support each other in setting and meeting individual development plans. Since you are both Accounting Technicians, you regard this as part of your Continuing Professional Development.

In order to gauge the effectiveness of this new scheme, the HR manager has asked you to prepare a short informal report, outlining:

a)   How you will help your Development Buddy to identify her training or learning needs

b)   What types of learning resources and opportunities you are aware of, that you might encourage your Development Buddy to try

c)   How you would go about evaluating and selecting a learning method for a particular competence that you wanted to develop.

chapter 4:
ETHICS FOR MEMBERS IN BUSINESS

chapter coverage 📖

'Members in business' may be salaried employees of an organisation or a volunteer working for a charity. They may be responsible for preparing and reporting financial and other information, which their employer and third parties may rely on. They may also be responsible for financial management and advice on a range of business-related matters.

In this chapter, we focus on the employer/employee relationship, and guidelines for professional conduct within an employing organisation.

The topics we shall cover are:

✍ The ethical organisation

✍ The employment relationship

✍ Threats and safeguards for members in business

✍ Integrity as an employee and colleague

✍ Conflicting loyalties

✍ Dealing with illegal or unethical conduct by an employer

KNOWLEDGE AND UNDERSTANDING AND PERFORMANCE CRITERIA COVERAGE

Knowledge and understanding

- The guidelines of your professional body
- A principle-based approach to professional ethics
- Legal considerations

Performance criteria – Element 32.2

- Describe the type of culture within organisations which supports and promotes high ethical values and helps resolve any conflict of loyalties

- Resolve conflicting loyalties where an employer may ask you to perform tasks which are illegal, unethical or against the rules or standards of the accounting profession

- Follow appropriate procedures where you believe an employer has committed or will commit an act which you believe to be illegal or unethical

- Respond appropriately to requests to work outside the confines of your own professional experience and expertise

THE ETHICAL ORGANISATION

Business ethics

The concept of **business ethics** suggests that businesses (and other corporate entities) are morally responsible for their actions, and should be held accountable for the effects of their actions on people and society. This is true for individual businesses (which should behave ethically towards the employees, customers, suppliers and communities who are affected by them) and for 'business' in general, which has a duty to behave responsibly in the interests of the society of which it is a part.

Ethical challenges for organisations

Managers have a duty (in most enterprises) to aim for profit. At the same time, modern ethical standards require them to protect the rights of a range of STAKEHOLDERS: groups (inside and outside the organisation) who have a legitimate interest or 'stake' in the organisation's activities.

So, for example, organisations have responsibilities to ensure that employees, visitors and members of the public are protected from danger on their premises, or in using their products or services. Attempts to increase profitability by cutting costs may lead to dangerous working conditions or to inadequate safety standards in products: the thrust of EU legislation has been to enforce ethical standards in this area.

Organisations are increasingly also being held accountable for the impacts of their business and investment practices on the economies of rural areas and developing nations, and on the environment and natural resources. Businesses which have a high profile for 'green' and socially just policies – such as The Body Shop – are creating a highly competitive brand. (This often also includes ethical employment policies, such as job security and working conditions above the legal minimum requirements.)

Business ethics are also relevant to competitive behaviour: there is a distinction between competing aggressively (as in the Cola 'Wars') and competing unethically (for example, by stealing competitors' designs; using buyer power to prevent suppliers from dealing with competitors; or spreading false negative information about competitors).

Activity 1

A company imports hand-made carpets from developing countries for sale in the UK. The company believes that it is preserving a craft, and benefiting communities. However, the carpets are typically made by children – and a recent TV documentary has focused public attention on the exploitation of child labour (by companies unrelated to this particular one).

What ethical issues arise for this company? (Use the 'critical decision-making' criteria covered in chapter 1, if you need to.)

Managing ethics

There are two basic approaches to managing ethics in organisations.

The **compliance-based** approach is mainly designed to ensure that the company acts within the letter of the law: violations are prevented, detected and punished. This may involve:

- Compliance procedures, to detect misconduct

- Systems for employees to report criminal misconduct without fear of retribution (ie protecting 'whistle blowers')

- Disciplinary procedures to deal with misconduct

While useful in preventing illegal behaviours (and protecting the company from the consequences), compliance is no guide to best practice ('the law is a floor'). Nor does it give managers and employees principles and skills which they can use to identify and solve ethical issues which are not directly covered by legal and ethical codes.

The **integrity-based** (or **principled**) approach combines a concern for the law with an emphasis on personal responsibility and decision-making in ethical behaviour. It focuses on encouraging people to develop strong ethical values and standards – and the critical decision-making skills to identify and resolve ethical issues as they occur. It makes ethics an issue of organisation culture, by:

- **Defining** and giving life to an organisation's core ethical values

- Creating an environment that **supports** ethically sound behaviour

- Promoting a sense of **shared moral accountability** among employees

Such an approach integrates ethical values into all the company's HR systems (using ethical criteria for employee selection, reward and promotion; setting ethical objectives for training and development; and so on). It also develops mechanisms for guidance and consultation on ethical issues, providing on-

student notes✍

going support for employees in identifying and resolving ethical dilemmas and problems.

Activity 2

Why might an integrity-based approach be more or less effective than a compliance-based approach in ensuring ethical behaviour in an organisation?

HOW IT WORKS

Your presentation on professional ethics to the Belgiorno Bellman trainees was so successful that you have been recommended to one of the firm's tax clients, to run a series of workshops on business ethics for its accounts departments.

The client is PodMore Ltd, a company specialising in the design, manufacture and sale of accessories for personal digital music players. The company has recently received some bad press on the Internet, in relation to the copying of designs and the alleged misuse of on-line customers' personal data. PodMore relies on its brand (and the support of Apple, whose resellers stock its i-Pod accessories), so it is implementing a comprehensive ethics management programme.

You have an introductory meeting with the PodMore accounts manager and section heads.

They describe a range of internal controls in place to ensure that there is little risk of employees committing or concealing fraud.

- Cash, cheques and other assets are kept under lock and key, and there are passwords for access to all data held on computer.

- Duties are segregated (eg the employee responsible for recording sales orders does not also maintain stock records), making it more difficult to falsify records and conceal fraud.

- All payments must be authorised by a section head.

You ask how employees are encouraged to develop high ethical standards – and how any ethical concerns are raised and resolved. The section heads tell you that they emphasise the need for honesty and the penalties for misconduct in the induction training given to all new employees. The same information is given in the office handbook. If employees have any ethical questions, they can raise them with their section head.

'What if the problem concerns the section head?' you ask. 'Or the firm as a whole?'

The section heads look at each other. 'It doesn't arise,' someone says eventually. 'I suppose we don't talk about ethics much. Not as such. The controls are in place – because we have to assume that people might be dishonest. We don't try to make them honest!'

You make a note:

- Workshop on individual ethical values

- Workshop on ethical questions, dilemmas, issues commonly encountered

- Report to management: need for ethics communication, arbitration?

Ethics and organisation culture

So what kinds of values support high standards of ethical behaviour in an organisation – and make it easier to resolve any ethical concerns or issues that may arise?

Openness. Makes it more likely that employees will feel able to talk with their superiors or mentors about any ethical concerns or issues they have

Trust. Sets a challenge to live up to expectation, by being trustworthy

Enables confidential discussion of concerns without fear of disclosure or exposure

Integrity. Establishes honesty, in conduct and communication, as an expectation and norm

Supports the raising of ethical issues by upholding integrity as a positive value (as opposed to a form of 'disloyalty')

Respect. Provides guidelines for constructive interpersonal relations, based on recognition of the value and rights of others

Establishes the basis for assertive and ethical communication styles

Empowerment. Gives employees the authority and skills to deal with work problems and issues – including ethical conflicts

Encourages employees to feel they have a stake in the shared objectives, reputation and standing of the enterprise (which they are committed to uphold through ethical conduct)

Accountability. Makes employees liable to be called to account if they fall short of ethical standards or legal compliance: acts as a safeguard/deterrent to unethical action and an incentive to make appropriate disclosures

Supports any disciplinary action that may have to be taken to rectify the problem

Encourages employees to take ethical and legal compliance seriously (encouraging responsible behaviour and co-operation in problem-solving)

Activity 3

Before reading on, how do you think these values can be established in an organisation?

HOW IT WORKS

After your first PodMore workshop on individual values, the accounts manager tells you that she was a bit disappointed. 'Not by your presentation – but by the low ethical awareness in our department. No-one seems to care much: they just do what the procedures require, in order to stay out of trouble.' She asks you how a company can develop high ethical values and standards. You promise to submit a written briefing.

Back in the office, you make notes.

Creating an ethical culture

1) Mission statement: clearly state concern for high standards .

2) Ethics objectives (eg to be in the Top 10 Ethical Brands within 5 years)

3) Ethical guidelines and/or statement of key values promoted to all staff

4) Include ethical values in all HR systems (not just disciplinary):

   – Recruitment literature and selection/interview criteria

   – Appraisal criteria + training needs analysis + merit-based rewards

   – Development/promotion plans

5) Ethics forums: eg employee ethics circles to discuss issues, and/or inclusion in joint consultation (union/staff) meetings

6) Resolution mechanisms (above statutory requirements): guarantee fair/confidential complaint/disclosure handling; ensure investigation/follow-up; non-punitive solutions were possible (eg counselling, training of offenders)

7) Top-down modelling: ethical values expressed and behaviours demonstrated by senior management; managers acknowledge/celebrate ethical behaviour by staff.

Signpost

See the *AAT Ethical Guidelines*:

- **Section 300**: Introduction (members in business)

THE EMPLOYMENT RELATIONSHIP

What does it mean to behave ethically in the employer-employee relationship? What are the two parties' obligations towards one another?

Again, we can take a compliance-based approach – or a principled approach.

The employment contract

There doesn't have to be a formal written contract of employment, but an employer is bound by law in the UK to provide a 'statement of written particulars on employment' (usually in the form of a letter), stating what has been agreed in regard to the job title and place of work, rates of pay, working hours, holiday entitlements, notice periods, sickness and pension provisions and disciplinary/grievance procedures.

These are the 'express' terms of the contract: they set out in detail what the organisation expects of the employee – and what the employee is entitled to expect in return. In addition, there are 'implied' terms arising from legislation on health and safety at work, equal opportunity and discrimination, employment protection and so on.

Employees have a fundamental general duty of **'faithful service'** to an employer:

- To give a 'fair day's work for a fair day's pay'
- To obey lawful and reasonable orders and instructions
- To use skill and care to protect the interests of the employer

Activity 4

Give two examples, covered earlier in this Companion, of unethical behaviour which would breach the duty of faithful service.

Employers, for their part, have a general legal duty to treat employees with due respect and consideration.

Any disputes between an employer and an employee can be taken to an Employment Tribunal.

The psychological contract

A PSYCHOLOGICAL CONTRACT is the set of **expectations** an employer and employee have of one another: how they subjectively define their relationship. This is not always the same as the legal contract of employment!

Traditionally, the psychological contract was one where the employer expected compliance and loyalty, and offered job security and career development in return. Nowadays, this is no longer possible – or necessarily desirable – in fast-changing business environments. Employers now often require values such as flexibility and value-adding performance – and, in return, offer opportunities for empowerment and self-development. Many are honest about the need for employees to take responsibility for their own careers.

The ethical approach is, from this point of view, about:

- Negotiating a fair and mutually acceptable exchange of benefits from the relationship ('a fair day's work for a fair day's pay')

- Making expectations explicit, so that both parties know where they stand (avoiding conflict from misunderstandings)

- Being honest and realistic about what can be offered (eg not promising long-term job security or promotion if this cannot be guaranteed)

THREATS AND SAFEGUARDS FOR MEMBERS IN BUSINESS

The following checklist may help you to identify and evaluate threats to the fundamental ethical principles which may arise in the course of employment. (See chapter 1 for explanation of threats and safeguards in general.)

Threat	Examples	Safeguards
Self interest	■ Having a financial interest (eg shares or a loan) in the employer ■ Financial incentives and rewards based on results or profits (including commission) ■ Opportunity to use corporate assets to your own advantage ■ Threats to your job security or promotion prospects ■ Commercial pressure (you need to help the firm compete and operate successfully, in order to keep your job)	■ Safeguards created by the profession, law and regulation (eg the AAT Ethical Guidelines or Money Laundering regulations) ■ The employer's structures and systems for corporate governance ■ The employer's own ethical codes and disciplinary processes, and training/communication about them ■ Internal controls ■ Quality/performance monitoring systems
Self review	■ Being asked to review data or justify/evaluate decisions that you have been involved in preparing/making	■ Recruitment, selection, appraisal, promotion, training and reward systems that all highlight ethics and competence as key criteria
Familiarity	■ Having a close or personal relationship with someone who may benefit from your influence on decisions or financial reports ■ Long association with a business contact, which may influence your decisions ■ Acceptance of a gift or preferential treatment which might be thought to influence your decisions	■ Leaders that communicate and model ethical behaviour and expectations ■ Policies and procedures supporting employees in raising ethical concerns ('whistle blowing') ■ Forums for discussing ethical issues at work (eg an ethics committee) ■ The opportunity to consult with another professional (in confidence) if required
Intimidation	■ Threat of dismissal or other sanctions over a disagreement or a matter of ethical principle ■ A dominant individual attempting to influence your decisions	

student notes ✐

student notes

Note that there is unlikely to be a significant **advocacy** threat: employees of an organisation are entitled and expected to promote the employer's position or viewpoint, as part of furthering its legitimate goals and objectives.

> ## Signpost
>
> See the *AAT Ethical Guidelines*:
>
> - **Section 300**: Threats and safeguards (300.7 – 300.17)

INTEGRITY AS AN EMPLOYEE AND COLLEAGUE

Professional competence and due care

You may be asked to undertake a wide range of tasks in the course of your work. Some of these tasks may be significant in their potential impact on the organisation and its stakeholders. And some of them may be tasks for which you have had little or no specific training or direct experience: tasks relating to a specialist field of accountancy, say, or to a specific industry sector or organisation type (such as charities) – or even unfamiliar software and systems.

Potential **threats** to the principle of competence and due care include: time pressure (when there may not be enough time to complete a task properly); insufficient or inaccurate information; lack of resources (eg equipment or help); or your own lack of experience, knowledge or training.

These threats may not be significant if you are working as part of a team, or under supervision, or on a comparativelylow-level task. If they *are* significant, however, you may need to apply safeguards.

Much as you may enjoy a 'challenge', take great care:

- Not to mislead your employer by stating (or giving the impression) that you have more knowledge, expertise or experience than you actually have!

- To state clearly and assertively that a particular task is outside the boundaries of your professional expertise and experience.

- To be realistic, responsible and proactive in requesting or accessing whatever extra time or resources, advice, help, supervision or training you need to deliver competent performance and to meet agreed deadlines.

If you can't get the time, information, resources or help you need to do the job properly, you may have to refuse to do it – explaining your reasons clearly or carefully to your boss.

Signpost

See the *AAT Ethical Guidelines*:

- **Section 330**: Acting with sufficient expertise

Financial interests

There are a number of ways in which an accountant could gain financially from his or her activities for an employer – and many of these might pose a **self-interest threat** to fundamental ethical principles such as integrity, confidentiality, or objectivity. We looked at a number of examples in Chapter 2, under the heading of fraud. Other potential threats might be where you, or someone close to you: holds a financial interest (eg a loan or shares), is eligible for a profit-related bonus; or holds, or is eligible for, share options in the employing organisation. The decisions and reports made or influenced by an accountant may affect the value of such interests (eg by inflating profit figures or enhancing share values).

If such threats are significant (ie the interest is direct and of high value), safeguards will have to be put in place. If you think there may be an issue, you should consult with your supervisor, and perhaps with higher authorities. The law and regulation on insider trading and corporate governance already provides some safeguards, such as: an independent committee to set remuneration (for senior managers); and the need to disclose relevant interests and share trading to the officials in charge of corporate governance in your organisation.

The bottom line is: don't **manipulate** information, and don't **use** confidential information, for your own financial gain!

Signpost

See the *AAT Ethical Guidelines*:

- **Section 340**: Financial interests

Inducements

We have already discussed the issue of gifts, hospitality and other 'inducements' or attempts to influence an accountant's decisions or actions, in Chapter 2. These may constitute:

- A **self-interest threat** to integrity, confidentiality or objectivity, if the inducement is made to encourage illegal or dishonest behaviour, to

student notes

obtain confidential information, or to influence the member's decisions.

- An **intimidation threat** – if an inducement has been accepted, and someone threatens to expose the member (potentially damaging his or her reputation and career).

Some appropriate safeguards include:

- Informing your boss if an offer (other than something clearly insignificant or customary) has been made

- Informing your boss if a close or personal relation of yours is employed by a competitor or potential supplier of your organisation (because an inappropriate appeal to your relationship, friendship or loyalty may be a form of 'inducement').

Look back at the 'Gifts and hospitality' and 'anti-corruption legislation' sections of chapter 2 if you need to.

> ## Signpost
>
> See the *AAT Ethical Guidelines*:
>
> - **Section 350**: Inducements

Preparing and reporting information

In chapter 2, we also mentioned that accountants have a key role in preparing **financial statements**. Members in business may also prepare and report on a range of **information** for use by management and/or outside bodies: forecasts and budgets, costings, pricing calculations, management/business reports and so on.

There is a clear need to update the principles of integrity (not presenting untruthful or misleading information), confidentiality (not disclosing confidential information), competence and due care (preparing and presenting information in accordance with financial reporting and other applicable professional standards) and objectivity (presenting information free of bias or self interest).

If you are induced or pressured to distort or withold information, there is a clear self-interest or intimidation threat. If you cannot reduce the threat (by safeguards such as consultation and reporting), you may have to refuse to be associated with the information – and (if the issue is persistent) to seek legal advice.

> ## Signpost
>
> See the *AAT Ethical Guidelines*:
>
> - **Section 320**: Preparation and reporting of information

Support for professional colleagues

Accounting matters often require the use of personal judgement – and opinions as to the best or 'right' way to handle them can sincerely differ. Moreover, people need to develop their own ethical and technical judgement, as part of their own personal and continuing professional development. So it is important for professionals, particularly those in positions of authority over others, to avoid handling differences of opinion in ways that undermine or discredit colleagues.

Where possible (that is, where a legal or ethical principle is not clearly at stake) try to allow your colleagues and subordinates to develop and express their own views and values – even if you think they are wrong!

Honesty

By now, this should go without saying, but it is easy to take an 'everyone does it' approach and slip into behaviour that is, in fact, dishonest (or even illegal).

> ## Activity 5
>
> List some examples of behaviours that would be considered dishonest for you as an employee in your work context – other than the obvious examples of financial fraud or theft discussed in chapter 2. Include an example of dishonest behaviour that the perpetrator might not even be aware was dishonest.

Using the work phone for personal calls and taking 'sick days' when you aren't sick are fairly common behaviours – and the organisation culture may have come to regard them as 'harmless' or even 'normal'. But they are still dishonest.

Working relationships and interactions

Ethical dealings with other people – in any work context – include values such as:

- **Fairness and respect.** UK law prohibits discrimination and harassment on a variety of grounds, including race and colour, sex and sexual orientation, and religious belief. More generally, the increasing diversity of the modern workplace requires fairness, mutual respect and open communication, as the basis for constructive working relationships.

- **Respect for confidentiality and privacy.** Employers have specific duties to respect the confidentiality of employee information, but this should be extended to individual relationships – particularly if you have authority over others (and may be involved in counselling, disciplinary or grievance interviews).

- **Health and safety.** All employees have a general duty to behave in ways that contribute to, and maintain, a healthy and safe workplace. Reckless behaviour endangers both yourself and others: creating the risk of accidents, fire, security breach and so on.

HOW IT WORKS

At your second PodMore workshop, where you are getting the accounts staff to discuss their ethical questions and concerns, things get interesting!

- One accounting technician feels it is dishonest to use work time and systems for personal e-mails. Another argues that this is part of the 'psychological contract' at PodMore: staff get paid slightly under market rate, so it's understood that small 'perks' can be taken advantage of, as long as the system isn't abused. Lively discussion ensues as to where the line is between 'use' and 'abuse'.

- The first speaker accuses the other of dishonesty. You intervene and emphasise that no blame can be attached, since this has been a 'grey area' in the firm. Later, you take the accuser aside privately, and suggest that he gives some thought to the ethics of publicly criticising a professional colleague.

- One sales ledger clerk compares PodMore's ethics favourably to those of his previous employer, and begins to detail its attempts to infringe copyright. You intervene, and remind him that he owes a duty of confidentiality to his former employer.

- There is some discussion about workplace humour. A cost accountant has been hurt by constant jokes about his Jewish headgear and dietary observances. The others tell him to 'lighten up: Jewish jokes have been around for ever.' You draw the group's attention to the 2003 regulations on religious harassment. The group grows thoughtful…

- Later, one of the staff approaches you and says that he has an ethical dilemma. He exaggerated his past work experience on his CV when applying for the job, and wasn't questioned on it in the interview. Now, however, he is being given tasks which he is not sure he is competent to perform correctly – but is afraid that if he says anything, he will be accused of getting the job under false pretences and fired. You advise him to speak honestly with his supervisor – or at least to own up to being 'rusty' in this area: the important thing is not to take on tasks beyond his ability, and to get the help he needs.

CONFLICTING LOYALTIES

If you are an employed member of a professional body, or a 'member in business', you owe a duty of loyalty to your employer and to your profession. The AAT Guidelines state clearly that: 'A member in business has a responsibility to further the legitimate aims of their employing organisation. [Professional ethical codes] do not seek to **hinder** a member in business from fulfilling that responsibility, but consider circumstances in which conflicts may be created with the duty to comply with the fundamental principles'.

Where does your duty lie?

As an employee, your first duty will generally be to contribute to your organisation's objectives (ends), and to comply with all reasonable instructions, requests, rules and procedures (means) designed to further them. But what if some of these ends or means are unethical (as defined by the standards of your profession)? Where does your primary duty lie?

Your employer cannot legitimately require you to:

- Break the law

- Break the rules and standards of the accounting profession

- Put your name to, or otherwise be associated with, a statement which significantly misrepresents facts (particularly in connection with financial statements, tax or legal compliance).

- Lie to or mislead regulators or the firm's internal or external auditors

- Facilitate, or be part of, the handling of unethical or illegal earnings (ie Money Laundering)

The law and rules and standards of your profession take clear priority in such a conflict of loyalties: your duty is to refuse to obey the instruction or rule, unless it can be shown that it is not, after all, incompatible with legal and professional requirements.

student notes✍

This may be easier said than done, particularly if you are a junior employee and are being put under pressure by an influential (or personally overbearing) superior. You may need all your assertive communication techniques!

At the same time, it is worth remembering that not every difference of opinion on ethical issues is an ethical conflict – and not every ethical conflict is significant enough to present a real conflict of loyalties. In other words, pick your battles wisely!

Procedures for handling conflicting loyalties

There may or may not be formal internal procedures for dealing with ethical conflicts: they may be part of the organisation's grievance or conflict resolution procedures (which may be set out in an employee handbook or procedures manual). These will generally involve the following steps.

Step 1   Raise your concerns with your immediate superior where possible. Differences in view should be discussed as objectively and openly as possible, with a view to clearing up any misunderstandings – and perhaps mobilising the superior to use his or her influence in your support. Minor issues should be resolvable at this level.

Step 2   If the issue is significant and unresolved (or if it concerns the immediate superior), it should be taken to a higher level of management, and/or to the organisation's Ethics Committee.

At this level, you may have to make it clear that if the problem persists, you will be unable to continue as an employee: this may finally convince the employer of the need to do the right thing.

Step 3   If no other resolution proves possible, you may be forced to resign – although it is important to protect yourself with appropriate legal advice before doing so.

Step 4   Keep accurate, dated records of all meetings, discussions and correspondence in relation to any of the above measures, and of any independent or professional advice you receive on the matter. (This may be needed to protect your legal interests if there are further consequences of your, or your employers', actions.)

Bear in mind that, while you may seek confidential, independent or professional counselling and advice – and you should certainly explain the reasons for your resignation to your employer (eg in a letter or exit interview) – you are still bound by your duty of confidentiality. Unless you have a legal or professional duty to disclose the matter to appropriate authorities, this may prevent you from telling others about the issue, or about your reasons for leaving.

Activity 6

What is a 'grievance procedure'? Why is it important for an organisation to have a formal grievance procedure?

DEALING WITH ILLEGAL OR UNETHICAL CONDUCT BY AN EMPLOYER

In addition to ethical conflicts directly affecting your own work, you may become aware that your employers have committed (or may be about to commit) an act which you believe to be illegal or unethical.

Examples include:

- Various forms of fraud (as discussed in chapter 2)

- Falsification of records, or the supply of information or statements which are false or misleading

- The offer of inducements to influence external parties (such as government officials) who have power to help or hinder the employer's operations. This may take the form of bribes (payments made to secure services to which a company is not legally entitled) or 'grease money' (payments made to speed up services which are being stalled or obstructed). 'Gifts' are more problematical (particularly in some cultures, where they are regarded as part of civilised negotiation), but they are unethical if their intent is to influence decisions in the company's favour (eg to win a contract).

- The acceptance of inducements to help or hinder the interests of others, or to compromise objectivity and impartiality. For example, clients may offer inducements to collude in fraud or money-laundering, to overlook financial irregularities and so on.

- Other illegal activity – from health and safety violations, to money-laundering, to breach of copyright, sexual discrimination or misuse of personal data.

Your aim in dealing with such a situation is, initially, to persuade your employer not to initiate or complete the act, or to put things right and/or to change its policies and controls to ensure that the problem does not occur again. (The illegal or unethical acts may be taken by staff members or agents who have misused their delegated authority, contrary to organisational policies and intention: the organisation is still responsible.)

Again, there may be specific machinery to facilitate this process, or you may have to report the matter to successive levels of management with the power of decision-making in relevant areas.

student notes✎

There may be an ethics committee in the organisation: a group of executives (perhaps including non-executive directors) appointed to oversee company ethics and to make rulings on allegations of misconduct.

HOW IT WORKS

One of your PodMore workshop participants, a payroll clerk, approaches you and asks if you can give her some personal advice. You say that you will try to help – if you can – on the understanding that you cannot take responsibility.

It appears that the production department has been tipped off that a Health and Safety Inspector will be visiting the factory in a couple of days, following a complaint. Apparently, the factory supervisors are busy replacing safety guards on machinery, and covering up torn flooring – and generally disguising potential safety hazards. Now the production manager has asked the payroll clerk for a management report on sickness and injury pay, but the specific parameters he has set for the information will make it look as if there have been fewer and less serious accidents than has in fact been the case.

At this point, you stop the clerk and say that it would be inappropriate for you to hear more, but in your opinion this may be a genuine ethical conflict (if all the facts are true), as she is apparently being asked knowingly to present a misleading report. You advise her to speak in the first instance to her own supervisor, stating her concerns and asking the supervisor to take the matter up with the production manager.

Whistle blowing

WHISTLE BLOWING is the disclosure by an employee of illegal or unethical practices by his or her employer. Theoretically, this ought to be welcomed as in the public interest – but remember: confidentiality is also a very strong value in the accountant's code of ethics.

This is an important issue, because:

a) You are in a position to uncover information that you may feel requires disclosure.

b) You may be the one who is given information by a concerned employee or whistleblower.

In the UK, the Public Interest Disclosure Act 1998 offers some protection to employees, ensuring that they cannot be dismissed for disclosing otherwise confidential information internally, or to an appropriate regulator, if they do so in good faith and have reasonable grounds to believe:

■ That a criminal offence has been committed, is being committed or is likely to be committed

■ That the health or safety of any individual has been, is being or is likely to be endangered

■ That the environment has been, is being or is likely to be damaged and/or

■ That information on any of the above has been, is being or is likely to be deliberately concealed.

A public disclosure is a much trickier proposition! In such a case, you should obtain independent legal advice.

The most ethical approach may be to encourage and use available lines of communication within the company – so that there is less need to whistleblow externally.

Activity 7

If you begin to suspect that some of your employer's revenue comes from a criminal organisation, what should you do?

Signpost

See the AAT's separate guidance notes:

■ *The Ethics of Whistle blowing*

Downloadable from the AAT website: www.aat.org.uk.

Responsibility for detecting and preventing fraud

In a limited company, or plc, it is the responsibility of the company **directors** to prevent and detect fraud, by:

■ ensuring that the **activities** of the business are conducted honestly and that its **assets** are safeguarded;

■ establishing arrangements to **deter** fraudulent or other dishonest conduct and to **detect** any that occurs

■ ensuring that, to the best of their knowledge and belief, financial information, whether used internally or for financial reporting, is reliable.

It is the responsibility of an **external auditor** to:

■ Express an opinion on whether the financial statements give a true and fair view of the company's financial situation and results. If they are thought to be affected by fraud or error, the report should be qualified accordingly.

student notes

- Design audit procedures so as to have a 'reasonable expectation' of detecting misstatements arising from fraud or error

- Document any findings which indicate that fraud and error may exist, and report them to management. (If the matter needs to be reported to an appropriate authority, in the public interest, they request that the directors make the report. If the directors do not do so, or if the fraud casts doubt upon the integrity of the directors, the auditors should make the report themselves.)

> **Signpost**
>
> See the *AAT Ethical Guidelines*:
>
> - **Section 300**: Threats and safeguards applying to members in business
>
> - **Section 310**: Potential ethical conflicts and dilemmas

CHAPTER OVERVIEW

- The concept of business ethics suggests that businesses and other corporate entities are morally responsible for their actions.

- There are two basic approaches to managing ethics in organisations: a compliance-based approach (based on ensuring that the company acts within the letter of the law) and an integrity-based approach (based on developing ethical values and stimulating discussion and resolution of ethical issues)

- High standards of ethical behaviour are supported by cultural mechanisms which promote values such as: openness, trust, integrity, respect, empowerment and accountability.

- Employees and employers have contractual obligations towards each other, as defined by express and implied contract terms, and general duties in the employment relationship. In addition, the psychological contract may define their understanding of what each 'owes' the other.

- Key issues in being an ethical employee and colleague include: not undertaking tasks which are beyond your personal experience and expertise; not undermining your professional colleagues; honesty; and ethical relationships.

- In any conflict of loyalties, the requirements of the law and your professional standards take precedence – although you should use your judgement as to whether they will be seriously compromised enough to take action through grievance or ethics procedures.

- If you suspect that your employers have committed or may commit an illegal or significant unethical act, your first aim is to persuade them to stop or to put the matter right. If they do not, you may have to make a disclosure to an appropriate regulator – but you should seek independent legal advice.

HOW MUCH HAVE YOU LEARNED?

1   What is the difference between a 'bribe' and 'grease money'?

2   In what circumstances are you protected from dismissal as a result of disclosing otherwise confidential information about your employer?

3   Who has the main responsibility for preventing and detecting fraud?

4   List five values that support high standards of ethical behaviour in an organisation, and make it easier to resolve ethical issues.

5   If you are asked to do something that is outside your personal experience or expertise, you should attempt to conceal your concerns, as they would damage the reputation and standing of your profession. True or false?

6   You are employed in the accounts section of firm which is updating its employee handbook. You have been asked to write guidelines for fellow professional staff on the procedure to follow if there is conflict between the instructions/requests of the firm and the rules and standards of your profession.

    Prepare brief guidelines, indicating:

    a)   the kinds of conflicts that would trigger action; and
    b)   a procedure to follow.

7   Give one example each of:

    a) a self interest threat,
    b) a familiarity threat and
    c) an intimidation threat for a member in business.

8   Suggest how

    a) recruitment and
    b) the leadership of an organisation can act as a safeguard against threats to ethical behaviour.

chapter 5:
ETHICS FOR MEMBERS IN PRACTICE

chapter coverage 📖

In this chapter, we focus on the framework of, and specific situations that may be encountered in, public practice, or when providing accounting services as a self-employed person.

AAT members who provide accounting, taxation and related consultancy services on a self-employed basis in the UK must register on the scheme for self-employed members and comply with specific Guidelines and Regulations. However, they must also abide by the AAT's *Guidelines on Professional Ethics*, as covered here.

The topics we shall cover are:

- 🖎 Marketing professional services

- 🖎 Contracting to supply services

- 🖎 Fees and other remuneration

- 🖎 Changes in appointment

- 🖎 Handling clients' money

- 🖎 Maintaining professional independence

- 🖎 Conflict of interest

- 🖎 Professional liability

- 🖎 Ownership and lien

KNOWLEDGE AND UNDERSTANDING AND PERFORMANCE CRITERIA COVERAGE

Knowledge and understanding

- The guidelines of your professional body – including professional liability and negligence
- A principle-based approach to professional ethics
- Legal considerations: UK or own country

Performance criteria – Element 32.2

- Prepare appropriate letters of engagement and develop and implement a fair fees policy for your professional services

- Identify and explain how specific situations can undermine professional independence

- Prepare a policy to be followed for handling clients' monies

- Maintain independence and objectivity and impartiality in a range of circumstances

- Make recommendations for a policy statement in relation to a client wishing to change accountant

- Identify the scope of professional liability

- Prepare clear guidelines which should be followed to advertise your accounting services in a professional and ethical manner

- Give advice to clients on retention of books, working papers and other documents

THREATS AND SAFEGUARDS FOR MEMBERS IN PRACTICE

The following checklist may help you to identify and evaluate threats to fundamental ethical principles which may arise in the course of work in practice. (See chapter 1 for explanation of threats and safeguards in general.)

Threat	Examples	Safeguards
Self interest	■ Having a financial interest in the client (eg shares or a loan) ■ Depending substantially on fees from a given client ■ Having a close business relationship with a client ■ Concern about the possibility of losing the client's business ■ Contingent fees (based on specific finding or result being obtained from financial reporting)	■ Safeguards created by the profession, legislation or regulation (eg Financial Reporting Standards) ■ **Firm/practice-wide** safeguards (as for members in business) ■ Policies and procedures to monitor interests/relationships between the firm or engagement team and clients ■ Policies and procedures to monitor dependence on fees from major clients
Self review	■ Reporting on the effectiveness of financial systems you helped to design or implement ■ Reviewing records generated from data you prepared ■ Reporting on matters for which you have been responsible as an employee, officer or director of the client firm ■ Performing a service for a client (eg consultancy) which directly affects the results you are called on to evaluate or report	■ Using different teams, with separate reporting lines, where conflicts of interest or self-review may arise (sometimes called 'building Chinese walls') ■ **Engagement-specific** safeguards such as: – Consulting an independent third-party – Discussing ethical issues with the client – Involving another firm to perform, re-perform or review part of the assignment – Rotating senior personnel

Threat (cont)	Examples (cont)	Safeguards (cont)
Familiarity	■ You have a close or personal relationship with a director or officer in the client firm ■ You are offered (or accept) gifts or preferential treatment which might be thought to influence you ■ There is a long association between senior personnel in the practice and the client firm	■ **Client** safeguards (although these should not be relied on): – Competent individuals to make managerial decisions (not being unduly influenced) – Procedures to ensure objective decisions about engaging an accountancy firm – Corporate governance structure in place to oversee the engagement
Intimidation	■ Threat or dismissal or replacement from the client engagement ■ Threat of court action (litigation) ■ Pressure (eg to reduce fees by 'cutting corners' on the work)	
Advocacy	■ Promoting the shares of a financial statement audit client ■ Acting as an advocate of a client in court cases or disputes	

> ## Signpost
>
> See the *AAT Ethical Guidelines*:
>
> - **Section 200**: Introduction (for members in practice)
>   Threats and safeguards (200.5 – 200.17)
>
> Note that a distinction is made in the guidelines between:
>
> - 'Assurance' engagements, clients and teams – where the accountant(s) **express a conclusion** designed to enhance the confidence of intended users (other than the person responsible for the subject matter) about the outcome of the evaluation. Examples include auditing of financial statements, and reporting on the effectiveness of internal controls.
>
> - 'Non assurance' engagements, clients and teams – other services, such as preparation of data or consultancy.
>
> The point is that for *assurance services*, the accountant or team must be – and be seen to be – **independent** of the client, in order to be able to express a conclusion, free of bias, conflict of interest or undue influence.

We will now look at a range of specific ethical isssues and contexts applying to members in practice.

MARKETING PROFESSIONAL SERVICES

Any business needs to be able to promote and advertise itself in order to obtain work – but how it advertises itself, and how it tries to win an advantage over its competitors, is an ethical issue.

The general principle is that a professional practice, and its individual members, need to:

- Project an image consistent with the 'dignity' (the high ethical and technical standards) of the profession.

- Maintain integrity in all promotional actions and statements.

The content of advertisements

Advertising standards. All advertisements (plus promotional materials, letterheads and other documents issued by the practice) should comply with the law and Codes of Practice in regard to the honesty, truthfulness, clarity, decency and legality of their content.

Fees. If fees are mentioned in promotional material, ensure that the statements are not misleading eg about what is covered and how fees are calculated.

If you use low fees as a promotional tool, make sure that you can provide quality service for that price!

It is not unethical to offer a free consultation, at which fees will be discussed.

Advertising claims. Avoid claims which are subjective, difficult to prove or potentially misleading, particularly in regard to the size of the firm (what does 'the largest' refer to?) or the quality of the firm (can you really prove you're 'the best'?).

Affiliate and student members of the AAT must not specifically mention the AAT when advertising their services.

Competitor comparisons. Be careful if you compare your practice, services or fees to those of others. Such comparisons must be:

- Objective, factual and verifiable
- Relating to the same services (so as not to be misleading)

Disparaging statements. Do not make disparaging references to, or comparisons with, the practice or services of others – even if you think they are justifiable!

The requirement to be professionally dignified and not misleading also applies to the practice's **name**, **letter heading** and any **documents** used to communicate with clients and other parties (even the nameplates on the office door!). These matters are also subject to various legal provisions, concerning business names and designations, and the use of partners' and principals' names.

Activity 1

a) How might referring to your practice as 'the largest accountancy practice in the UK' be misleading?

b) How might the name of a practice be misleading?

Finding clients

'Aggressive' following up of contacts and leads is considered good marketing in some contexts – but it can be both counter-productive (putting clients off) and unethical if you are promoting professional services. If you contact or approach potential clients directly and repeatedly, or otherwise in a 'pushy' manner, you may be open to a complaint of **harassment**!

What about **recommendations and referrals**? A satisfied client may introduce others to your practice, and that's fine. You might also offer a commission, fee or reward to your employees for bringing in a new client. But you shouldn't offer financial incentives to a third party to introduce clients (a referral fee or commission) – unless:

- The client is aware that the third party has been paid for the referral; and

- The third party is also bound by professional (or comparable) ethical standards, and can be trusted to carry out the introduction with integrity.

In the UK, if you receive a **commission** for introducing a client to another firm, and you are the client's agent or professional adviser (regarded in UK law as a 'fiduciary relationship', or relationship of 'trust and confidence'), you are legally bound to hand the money over to the client – unless they specifically approve your keeping it.

And what if you've just left an employer: can you try to 'take clients with you' to your new practice? The Guidelines suggest only that you should act 'professionally and with integrity', using your own judgement – but bear in mind the bad will that is likely to result.

HOW IT WORKS

Back at Belgiorno Bellman, your work on professional ethics has been so helpful that one of your junior colleagues (Carla Jones) has asked you to mentor her as she plans to set up her own practice. The following are some of her more enthusiastic ideas for marketing her services.

- Carla wants to call her business 'Jones International'. You ask her how she can justify this, and she says that she has several personal tax clients who have moved overseas but are still retaining her services for their UK affairs. You tell her that you think the name may be misleading as to the size and scope of the business.

- Carla has drafted a short advertisement, in which her main selling point is her low fee rate. You advise Carla that she is certainly permitted to advertise – but that she should make sure that she is able to offer a suitable quality of service for the fees she is proposing to charge.

- Carla's business plan is based on her knowledge of the buy-to-rent housing market. As a property investor herself, she believes she has specialist knowledge to offer clients in this area, in relation to accounting for depreciation, claiming tax deductions and so on.

  'Can I advertise myself as a property finance specialist?' she asks. Only, you answer, if she genuinely has the expertise to justify the claim.

93

student notes

'I thought I'd offer a commission to local conveyancers and estate agents to introduce their clients to me,' she enthuses. You warn her that if she does this, she must ensure that the client is informed of the commission and that the conveyancers/agents carry out the introduction under ethical guidelines. You note that solicitors have a 'fiduciary relationship' with their clients, so any commission you pay them will have to be cleared by the clients – or transferred to them.

■   Her enthusiasm slightly dampened, Carla says: 'Well, at least I can be reasonably aggressive about following up leads and contacts, can't I?' You answer that it depends what she means by 'reasonably aggressive'. She means contacting them by e-mail, repeatedly if she hasn't heard back from them within a week – followed by telephoned requests for a meeting (if she can get hold of home or mobile numbers). You remind Carla not to contact people too frequently or persistently, at private numbers, or in a style that they might perceive as harassment.

Signpost

See the *AAT Ethical Guidelines*:

■   **Section 240**: Commission (240.5 – 240.9)
■   **Section 250**: Marketing professional services
■   **Section 253**: Names and letter heads of practices

Client acceptance procedures

Although we have so far dealt with a practice's desire to obtain clients, it is worth noting that, for various reasons, you may not want to take on every prospective client that approaches or is introduced to you!

Client acceptance procedures should take into account any ethical problems that may arise. For example, will you have the resources (staff, time, technical expertise) to give the client a quality service? Are there potential **threats** to objectivity (eg if you are related to an officer of the client company) or confidentiality (eg the client is a competitor of another client, and might pressure you to disclose information)?

The Money Laundering Regulations 2007 require you to exercise 'due diligence' in gathering information about a prospective client, including:

■   The client's **identity**, verified by appropriate identification and/or references – and the identity of the owner of the client (if separate)

■   'Know your client' (**KYC**) information, including its expected patterns of business, its business model and its source of funds.

Sufficient knowledge of a client must be maintained to enable you to identify unusual (and potentially suspicious) transactions. Where due diligence is not possible, you must decline to enter into relationship with the client. If you have any reasonable suspicion the client may be engaged in money laundering or terrorist financing, you must report to the MLRO of your firm (or SOCA, if you are a sole practitioner), as discussed in Chapter 2.

Activity 2

What forms of identification might be appropriate to verify the identity of

a) an individual and
b) a corporation?

CONTRACTING TO SUPPLY SERVICES

 Signpost

See the *AAT Ethical Guidelines*:

- **Section 210**: Professional appointment (Client acceptance: 210.1 – 210.6)

Constraints on the services you can supply

It is worth noting that as an accounting technician, there are certain services which you cannot legally offer unless you are authorised to do so by the relevant regulatory body in the UK. These include: external audit of UK limited companies, or where the services of a registered auditor are required; investment business (including agency for a building society) and the provision of corporate financial advice; and insolvency practice.

In addition, while you are providing public accountancy services, you should not at the same time engage in any other business, occupation or activity which:

- May threaten your integrity, objectivity or independence, or the reputation of the profession.

- May prevent you from conducting your practice according to the technical and ethical standards of the profession.

When considering accepting a particular engagement, you must also bear in mind any threat to the principle of professional competence and due care. You should only agree to provide services which you are competent to perform – or for which you can obtain the help, training or supervision you require in order to be able to perform competently.

student notes

Safeguards may include:

- Making sure that you have an adequate understanding of the client's business, and the specific requirements of the engagement.

- Making sure that you have, or can obtain, relevant knowledge and experience, help or advice

- Consulting an expert, if required

- Making sure the timescales for the task are realistic (so you are not under undue time pressure)

> ### Signpost
>
> See the *AAT Ethical Guidelines*:
>
> - **Section 210**: Engagement acceptance (210.7 – 210.9)

A contract for services

Members in public practice enter into a contract for services with a client, as defined in a contract or letter of engagement (see below). In forming this contract, the **member** takes on the legal responsibility to perform whatever assignment has been specified (a) with integrity and objectivity and (b) in accordance with appropriate technical standards. This is part of the accountant's implied duty of care, owed to the client under the Supply of Goods and Services Act 1982.

In return, the **client** undertakes to provide an agreed remuneration (in the form of professional fees or commission).

We will look at each of these mutual obligations in turn.

Letter of engagement

A LETTER OF ENGAGEMENT provides written confirmation of the agreement with the client as to the nature and scope of the work to be undertaken, and the responsibilities of both the client and the accountant in the relationship. It is very important in managing client expectations, minimising threats arising from client pressure – and avoiding misunderstandings and later conflicts!

Any time a new assignment is undertaken, or additional tasks are added to an assignment, or the terms of an engagement alter, a new letter of engagement should be submitted. Both parties sign copies of the letter, so that each has a signed agreement for its files.

The following elements are recommended in the AAT Guidelines for inclusion in a standard letter of engagement.

The assignment	The nature of the assignment
	Work to be undertaken (and tasks specifically not included, where relevant)
	Reports to be delivered (scope and format)
Time-frames	Start date (subject to access to information, if relevant)
	Length of the assignment (or date of reporting)
	If the assignment is recurring (eg monthly or annually)
	If the engagement is open-ended (to be terminated by the client)
Client responsibilities	For producing records and books (format, timing)
	For tax returns submitted (since the member is only acting as an agent for the client)
	For provision of full and accurate information
Charges	The basis, frequency and rate of charge for services rendered (including contingency fees if applicable)
	Treatment of expenses
	Billing arrangements
Ownership	Who owns books and records created in the assignment
	The member's policy on retention, destruction and return of records (where relevant)
Unpaid fees	Penalties for non-payment (eg: interest charged; cessation of work; and/or the member exercising LIEN over the client's books and records)
Third parties	Whether the client can share the work with third parties or use it for other purposes.
	Disclaimer of liability for other uses.

Example letters of engagement are available from the AAT's website at www.aat.org.uk/lettersofengagement.

student notes

Activity 3

In a letter of engagement:

a) Why might a disclaimer be necessary in regard to third parties using the information provided as part of the assignment?

b) Whose responsibility is it to provide full and accurate information?

HOW IT WORKS

A client previously told you informally that she expected to inherit from a recently deceased uncle. (You declined to advise her informally on inheritance tax, capital gains tax and other matters, since you were not sure of your expertise in these areas.) However, she has now received a considerable sum from the uncle's estate, and wants to consult you on 'the best thing to do with it'.

This amounts to investment advice – and you are not authorised to give it, under the Financial Services Act. You inform the client clearly of this, and she agrees to get this advice elsewhere. She says she would like you to calculate her tax liabilities in regard to the inheritance and any investment options.

This is not in your original letter of engagement, so you propose that you draw up a new one to cover the task. 'But it will still be included in the fee we agreed, won't it?' the client asks. You answer that the original fee was based on the estimated time it would take to complete specified tasks: since you need to ensure that you can give her quality service (and this new assignment will take you some time, as it is not your area of expertise), you feel that you should negotiate a fee for the additional work.

You draw up a letter of engagement for a non-recurring short-term assignment, specifically excluding the provision of investment advice. The assignment will be fulfilled by the submission of a letter of advice on the tax implications of her inheritance and investment options, for the agreed fee. It is the client's responsibility to provide relevant information on which to base your advice: she also takes full responsibility for decisions she takes as a result of that advice. Your advice is provided for this purpose only, and should not be relied upon by any other party or for any other purpose.

▶ Signpost

See the *AAT Ethical Guidelines*:

■ **Section 252**: Letters of engagement

FEES AND OTHER REMUNERATION

Fees policy

Professional fees will normally be calculated on the basis of an agreed appropriate **rate per hour or per day** for the time of each person involved on the assignment. The 'appropriate rate' should take into account the skill, knowledge, experience, time and responsibility involved in the work. (It also assumes that individuals give a 'fair hour's work for a fair hour's fees': in other words, that the work is efficiently planned and managed, so that clients get value for money...) Note that there may be a threat to the principle of professional competence and due care if fees are set too *low*: it may be difficult to do a good job for that price!

It may not be possible to state accurately in advance what the total charge for work will be. If there is any likelihood that the fee will end up being substantially higher than you estimate, don't give the clients that estimate – or at least make it clear that the actual amount may be substantially higher.

It may, however, be necessary to charge a **pre-arranged fee** for the assignment, based on your estimate of how long the work will take: this is quite acceptable, as long as the fee is fair for the work – and the work is fulfilled on that basis.

Contingency fees

CONTINGENCY (OR PERCENTAGE) FEES depend on the results of the services provided, usually in the form of a percentage of whatever money is gained on behalf of the client.

This is customary where professional help is required to gain the client funds (eg an asset realisation or distribution, or debt recovery): if the assignment is not successful, the client may not be able to pay – and therefore, a percentage fee, contingent on results, is the only way they could gain access to professional services.

Be aware, however, that you *can't* offer financial reporting services on a contingent fee basis, depending on a specific finding or result being obtained: this would present a major threat to your professional objectivity!

Expenses

Out-of-pocket expenses which are directly related to the work performed for a particular client (such as travelling expenses) may be charged to the client, for reimbursement, in addition to professional fees.

Activity 4

Give examples of when it would – and when it would not – be appropriate to offer services on a contingent fee basis.

Ethical remuneration policy

Safeguards to ensure ethical remuneration include:

- Agreeing the basis of payment with the client in advance

- Assigning sufficient time and qualified staff to the task to do a good job – and estimating fees accordingly

- Checking regulations and policies on contingent fees for certain types of engagement

HOW IT WORKS

You have just had a phone call from a prospective new client, asking about fees. You offer a free-of-charge consultation to discuss the matter. The client has recently left his job to become a freelance photographer: in the first instance, he requires an accountant to prepare financial statements and tax returns, and to advise on financial management.

'How much will you charge per year?' he asks. You explain that your fees are based on an hourly rate, which you quote to him.

'Yes, but how much in total?' he asks. You explain that it will depend on the work involved. You could make an estimate – but you would need authorisation from the partner to whom you report. Moreover, the client would have to be aware that the amount actually billed could be substantially higher: for example, if the client's business arrangements proved to be different from that anticipated.

'Do you reduce the fee if you don't save me as much tax as you thought?' the client asks. You explain that you cannot set a contingent fee on this basis: nor can you make any promises in relation to tax savings. 'What about if I get you to help me with a proposal for an Arts Grant that's available for photographers?' he persists. 'Will you accept a commission on that, instead of an hourly rate?' You agree that this would be possible.

'What about expenses?' pursues the client. 'Will I be paying for all this nice office space?' 'No', you explain. 'This is covered in our overall charge out rates; only out-of-pocket expenses directly related to your work for him will be charged.'

Signpost

See the *AAT Ethical Guidelines*:

■ **Section 240**: Fees and other types of remuneration

CHANGES IN APPOINTMENT

Change from one adviser to another

For all sorts of reasons, a client may wish to change from one professional adviser to another: (s)he may be relocating, or looking for more (or different) specialised expertise – or lower fees. Or the adviser may have died or retired!

Clients have the right to change advisers. The ethical issue is how to protect the interests of all parties, by ensuring that information relevant to the change of appointment is properly exchanged.

If you are **approached by a prospective client** to act for them in regard to a recurring reporting assignment, accounting services or tax compliance work, an appropriate procedure (building in safeguards) would be as follows.

Step 1   Explain to the client that you have a professional duty to communicate with their existing (or previous) adviser. If the client refuses permission for you to do so, you should decline to act for them.

Step 2   Request the client to notify the existing/previous adviser of the proposed change and to authorise them to co-operate with you as possible successor.

Step 3   Write to the adviser about his or her involvement with the client, requesting disclosure (on a confidential basis) of any issue or circumstance which might be relevant to your decision of whether or not to accept the appointment (eg if the adviser is in dispute with the client over a technical or ethical matter). This is called a 'professional clearance' letter.

Step 4   If no reply is received, write again (by Recorded Delivery) stating your intention to accept the appointment unless a reply is received within a reasonable specified period. (If there is still no reply, you are entitled to assume that there are no significant problems to be disclosed.)

Step 5   Decide whether you will accept or decline the appointment, or accept it once issues identified with the existing/previous adviser have been resolved. (The existing/previous adviser doesn't have any authority in this matter: you don't need his 'permission' to take over the client – but you should take his reply, and any other relevant information, into careful consideration.) This will also depend on customer due diligence (in regard to possible money laundering – as discussed in our section on 'Client acceptance' procedures).

Step 6 Draw up and submit a letter of engagement to your new client.

Step 7 Request from the previous adviser any books and papers which belong to the client – and any useful information that might be of help to you in serving the client's best interests.

Activity 5

a) How does the professional clearance process protect the interests of all parties (client, previous adviser and new/prospective adviser)?

b) What might be your inference if a client does not want you to obtain professional clearance or contact his previous accountants directly?

If you **receive a communication from a client**, saying that they want to transfer their business to another professional adviser, the appropriate procedure is as follows.

Step 1 Respond promptly to all communications on the matter from your proposed successors. (Stalling won't help you keep the client…)

Step 2 Disclose any issue or circumstance which might affect the successor's decision to accept the appointment – or confirm that there are no such issues.

In these circumstances, you may have to disclose matters which are damaging to the reputation of your client and any individuals concerned with their business. In UK law, this communication is generally protected by 'qualified privilege'. This means that you should not be liable if the client attempts to sue you for **defamation**. DEFAMATION depends on the malicious use of untrue statements to damage someone's reputation – so in making your disclosure, be sure to state only what you believe sincerely (and with reasonable grounds) to be true!

Another issue may arise if you suspect that the client is involved in money laundering: remember that you *cannot* make any disclosures which might be used to 'tip off' a possible money launder or terrorist.

Step 3 Once the change of appointment has been made, hand over books and papers promptly to your successor if asked to do so (although there may be an issue if you have exercised a lien over them, in pursuit of outstanding fees: we discuss this later).

Step 4   If your successor needs other information from you, in the client's interests, give it promptly (and without charge – unless it involves a significant amount of work).

Appointment of an additional adviser

If a client approaches you to undertake work which is additional and related to the work of an existing professional adviser, you should similarly notify the existing adviser about this – unless the client can provide acceptable reasons for not doing so.

If you don't communicate with the other adviser(s), there may be a risk of duplicated effort (at best) and fraudulent or otherwise illegal activity (at worst).

There may also be a threat where you are asked to provide a *second opinion* on work done by another firm. Professional competence may be an issue, for example, if you don't have access to the same information the other firm had. Again, getting permission to make contact with the other firm is one good safeguard.

HOW IT WORKS

The freelance photographer (Franklin Delaney) has decided to engage you as his accountant. It now turns out that he already has (or has had) a firm of accountants advising him – but that he wants to transfer his business to you.

You ask him to inform the previous firm that he is proposing to change advisers, and tell him that you have a professional duty to contact them directly. At first he is reluctant to give you their name and details, but you insist that this is the only basis on which you will consider the engagement. He finally agrees.

student notes

You write to the previous advisers.

> Bongiorno Bellman
> Chartered Accountants
> 24 Church Lane
> Barnt Green
> Birmingham B52 8WR
>
> Hopkirk & Co
> Accountants
> First Flr, 39 Abernathy Mews
> London SW10 4LL
>
> [Date]
>
> Dear Sirs,
>
> **Re: Franklin Delaney**
>
> We have been asked to act for the above individual, and we should therefore be grateful if you would let us know at your earliest convenience, whether there are any professional reasons why we should not accept this request.
>
> Any information provided will be handled in the strictest confidence (subject to law, regulation or professional guidelines).
>
> Thank you for your kind attention.
>
> Yours faithfully,
>
>
> *Your Name*
>
>
> Accounting Technician
> Belgiorno Bellman

You receive a letter from Hopkirk & Co some days later, stating that the only matter which, in their opinion, might give you concern, is that Mr Delaney is not up-to-date in his payment of fees to them. You consider carefully whether this, in itself, is a sufficient reason not to act for Mr Delaney – and, after consultation with Sheila, decide that it isn't.

▶ Signpost

See the *AAT Ethical Guidelines*:

- **Section 210**: Professional appointment / Changes in a professional appointment (210.10 – 210.19)

- **Section 230**: Second opinions

HANDLING CLIENTS' MONEY

When not to hold clients' monies

You should not hold clients' monies if:

- They are the monies of investment business clients (under the UK Financial Services Act 1986), and you are not regulated under relevant authorisation schemes

- There is reason to believe that they are 'criminal property' (obtained from, or to be used for, criminal activities): this would constitute money laundering, as discussed in chapter 2.

Policy for handling clients' monies

Separation – Clients' monies should be kept separately from monies belonging to you personally and/or to the practice

Separate bank accounts should be maintained for clients' monies: whether a general client account or separate accounts in the name of each client. When opening such an account, the bank should be notified in writing of the nature of the account, and acknowledgement requested. (This should protect your clients' money if you go bankrupt.)

Use – Clients' monies should be used only for the purpose for which they are intended

Monies received should be promptly deposited (and related documents, such as share certificates or title deeds, secured) to avoid unauthorised use.

Monies should only be drawn from the client account on the client's instruction, or for the benefit of the client. (You cannot draw on the account for payment of your fees unless the amount has been clearly agreed by the client.)

The client account should be responsibly managed. It should never be overdrawn. If more than £2,000 is likely to remain in the account for more than two months, you should (with the client's agreement) place the money in a separate interest bearing account: all interest should then be credited to the client.

Accountability – You must be ready at all times to account for the monies to authorised enquirers

Keep accurate and up-to-date account books, so that you can establish exactly what you have done with the monies at all times. Statements of account should be provided to clients at least once a year.

Services that involve handling client's money raises the risk of involvement in money laundering, and so require a higher level of client identification and 'Know Your Client' procedures. The Money Laundering Regulations 2003 recommend verifying the identity of the client, the commercial purpose of the transaction and the source and destination of the funds.

Activity 6

Outline a policy which ensures that client accounts are managed in the best interests of the client.

HOW IT WORKS

Franklin Delaney, your new client, phones to ask if you would hold some money on his behalf, 'for reasons he would rather not discuss at the moment'. Although you have carried out due diligence in confirming Mr Delaney's identity and sources of income, you explain to him that you cannot hold any client's monies without verifying the commercial purpose of the transaction and the source and destination of the funds.

Meanwhile, another client has deposited funds with you pending completion on a house purchase: the client will be overseas at the time, and you have agreed to liaise with her solicitor to complete the transaction. It is agreed that your own fees may be drawn from the client account.

 ## Signpost

See the *AAT Ethical Guidelines*:

■ **Section 270**: Custody of client assets

MAINTAINING PROFESSIONAL INDEPENDENCE

Objectivity is a vital principle of professional integrity – as we saw in chapter 1 – and is particularly important in **financial reporting** and similar 'assurance services', where independence of mind and in appearance is necessary to enable the member to express a conclusion which is (and can be seen to be) free of bias, conflict of interest or undue influence of others.

Before you decide to accept a new appointment or engagement (or to continue with an existing one), you need to consider:

■ Potential **threats to objectivity** which may arise – or appear to arise – from the context and/or the people connected with the work.

■ What **safeguards** can be put in place to offset the threats – and whether these are sufficient to protect your objectivity (and hence independence).

We have already summarised these, but will draw out some of the implications here.

Threats to objectivity and independence

Most threats to your objectivity will arise from some type of involvement by you (or someone closely connected to you) in a client's affairs.

Self-interest. You (or those closely connected to you) are financially involved in a client's affairs, and may therefore be reluctant to take actions that would have an adverse affect on them.

For example, you have a significant financial stake (such as shares) in the client; you have made a loan to (or accepted a loan from) the client; or the clients' fees (from all services provided to the client) represent a large proportion of your total gross fees.

This is usually an 'insurmountable' threat to the appearance of objectivity.

Self-review. You have been operationally or managerially involved in the affairs (or preparation of accounts) which you are being asked to review or report.

For example, If you have been involved in maintaining the accounting records, or undertaking valuations, that will be incorporated in the financial statements.

If you have (within the past two years) been a **director, officer or employee** of the client company, you should not undertake a financial reporting (assurance) assignment in relation to the company.

In a **consultancy** (non-assurance) capacity, you should not report on management decisions which you have recommended, or go beyond a purely 'advisory' role in the client's managerial or tax decisions.

Familiarity. You have built up an emotional commitment to, or trust in, the client, and may therefore be inclined to accept their point of view too readily.

For example, you should not undertake financial reporting on behalf of a client with whom you have a family connection (spouse, dependant child or relative who lives with you) or other close business or personal relationship.

Intimidation. You are threatened or pressured by clients.

For example, you encounter an aggressive or dominating individual. (Hopefully, this will be rare – but it does happen!)

student notes✍

Advocacy. You have strong views in support of the client, particularly in a conflict situation.

For example, you support the position taken by a client in a court case, or in the Press.

Activity 7

You are the practice manager of a regional office of a large national firm of accountants. Revenue in your office represents 18% of the firm's income. Your office has two major clients, whose recurring fees constitute 30% and 40% of the office's annual income. This year, undertaking a special project for the latter client will take the total income from the client to your office to 60% of the year's income.

Comment on any issues this raises with regard to the independence of the firm.

Safeguards against threats to objectivity

Legal provisions and professional regulations are designed to reduce threats to objectivity and independence in some cases: a partial solution is therefore to comply with the rules!

Other safeguards include:

- Education and training, as a requirement for entry into (and continuing development within) the profession

- Policies and procedures for client acceptance and review, which take account of ethical issues

- Quality controls, and internal audits of quality controls, on reporting

- Mechanisms to empower and protect staff who raise concerns over independence or objectivity

- Involvement of, or consultation with, independent third parties (eg non-executive directors or regulatory bodies)

- Rotation of senior personnel (where possible) to avoid increasing familiarity with the client

- Transparency about the recognition and management of potential conflicts in a given situation

Activity 8

What is the final safeguard, if no other safeguard will reduce the risk?

Signpost

See the *AAT Ethical Guidelines*:

- **Section 280**: Objectivity – all services
- **Section 290**: Independence – assurance engagements

CONFLICT OF INTERESTS

When you accept a new appointment, or become aware of changes in the circumstances of an existing client, it is worth checking whether this might create a conflict of interests with another client. The general principle is that the interests of one client must not have a negative effect on the interests of another.

An example would be if two client companies are in direct competition – and adverse disclosures or reports about one would benefit the other. Such conflicts create an ethical dilemma for the accountant, because it is impossible to act in the best interests of both clients at the same time. It may also be an issue for a client, eg if they think there may be a risk that that another client may (through the accountant) get hold of sensitive information.

If there is likely to be such a conflict of interest, you should:

- Put safeguards in place to avoid the negative effects, if possible

- Avoid new appointments that might negatively affect existing clients

- Disclose enough information to both parties, so that they can make a decision over whether to enter into (or continue) an engagement with you.

In large firms, this may be less of a problem, as completely separate teams may work on different client accounts. (This is sometimes called 'building a Chinese wall' within the firm, between client affairs.)

HOW IT WORKS

It's another complicated week at Belgiorno Bellman!

Incident one

A long-term client wishes to renew your engagement for another year. However, you are aware that this client currently owes Belgiorno Bellman significant fees (arising from work done by various offices of the firm in various capacities) and has done so for a considerable time.

You ask Sheila whether the client is worth taking on again. 'That's not really the issue' Sheila replies. 'I hadn't realised they had owed us so much for so long. That's technically equivalent to our making them a loan of that amount – and that's a threat to objectivity and independence! It counts as a financial stake in the success of their business. I don't see how we can continue to act for them.'

Incident two

Meanwhile, you get a phone call from your sister, who announces with delight that she has just accepted a job with the property developer who is another one of your clients. You realise that this will create a threat to your objectivity, through personal relationship with the firm. You disclose the personal interest to Sheila, who says that she will disclose it to the property developer on behalf of Belgiorno Bellman. Sheila agrees to monitor the situation, to ensure that the natural safeguards of your personal integrity and professional standards (plus her own monitoring of your work) are sufficient to ensure objective work.

Incident three

Your travel agent client has been doing well – but you have now heard that another of your clients, a small national airline, is planning to open its own travel agency in direct competition. There is clearly going to be a conflict of interest between the two clients.

You discuss the matter with Sheila, who proposes to create a Chinese wall by handing the airline client to another partner at one of Belgiorno Bellman's other offices: no staff will be involved with both clients. She instructs you to inform both clients of the conflict, and the proposed safeguards, requesting their consent. After consideration, both clients agree.

You insert a paragraph into a new engagement letter, stating that 'all information will be kept confidential except as required by law, regulatory or ethical guidance, and the client permits the firm to take such steps as the firm thinks fit to preserve confidentiality.'

Signpost

See the *AAT Ethical Guidelines*:

- **Section 220**: Conflicts of interest

PROFESSIONAL LIABILITY

Members may be liable (open to legal action and payment of damages) on a number of grounds: criminal acts, breaches of trust, breaches of contract or statutory liability (eg for workplace accidents). However, the AAT's ethical guidelines only deal specifically with liability arising from **professional negligence**.

As we noted in chapter 1, you have a contractual **duty of care** to your clients: a duty to carry out your professional work with due skill, care, efficiency and timeliness, with proper regard for the technical and professional standards expected of you. Lack of understanding or knowledge on your part is not a legitimate excuse (or legal defence) for giving a client incorrect advice!

If you – or an employee or associate – do something (or fail to do something) which results in financial loss to a person to whom a duty of care is owed, you may incur liability for professional negligence. This can result in claims for substantial damages!

Documents often include a clause **disclaiming liability** (along the lines of: 'No responsibility can be accepted for …'). This may provide extra transparency for clients as to the need to exercise caution in relying on advice, but they can't be relied on as a legal protection from liability: courts may regard them as an attempt to wriggle out of legitimate responsibility.

Basic safeguards are as follows.

Step 1   Ensure that the exact scope of your duties (what specific matters are included and NOT included) is set out in your contract or letter of engagement to the client.

Step 2   If any additional duties or services are undertaken at a later date, ensure that these, too, are defined in writing.

Step 3   Ensure that the client is aware of the limitations and constraints which affect your advice (especially if the advice requested is informal or based on incomplete information).

              The same applies to unaudited accounts or financial statements submitted to clients. These should clearly state that they are confidential, unaudited and prepared solely for the private use of the client.

student notes

Step 4   Disclaim liability where it is legitimate to do so.

Step 5   Ensure that you have adequate Professional Indemnity Insurance to cover your potential liability (as set out in the scheme for self-employed members).

Step 6   If an assignment presents particularly complex or heavy liability issues, seek specialist legal advice – or advise the client to do so.

Activity 9

How can you protect yourself if a client asks you to advise on matters which are not within your current professional expertise?

HOW IT WORKS

A short while ago, you were asked by an estate agent to provide a financial reference for a client who was looking to enter into a rental agreement. Having checked with the client, you drafted the reference and sent it to Sheila for approval. Sheila has now sent back an amended copy, asking you to add the following items:

- The enclosed reference has been prepared without an audit

- The enclosed reference has been prepared from information, records and explanations supplied by the client

- Belgiorno Bellman disclaims all financial responsibility for the reference, or for decisions taken in relying upon the information provided.

Signpost

See the *AAT Ethical Guidelines*:

- **Section 257**: Professional liability of members

OWNERSHIP AND LIEN

Ownership of books and records

The ownership of books and records is mainly determined by **law** (check the position in your own country, if not the UK), but specific rights and responsibilities may also be as agreed in the **contract** (or letter of engagement) between the parties.

In common law, ownership also depends on the **capacity** in which you act for the client.

- If you are acting as a **principal** (and not as an agent) for the client, documents and records prepared, acquired or created by you, for your own purposes, belong to you. Only documents which have been created by you on the specific instructions of the client belong to the client.

- If you are acting as an **agent** for the client, documents will generally belong to the client.

In accounting work, the **purpose** of the documents and records is also relevant.

- Accounting records and financial statements prepared for a client belong to the client. Your working papers belong to you.

- In taxation work, documents normally belong to the client.

- Written advice and supporting papers (on tax, investment or other matters) given to a client belong to the client – but your working papers belong to you.

- Letters which you receive from the client, copies of letters you send to the client and your notes on discussions with the client all belong to you.

- Letters exchanged with third parties belong to you if you are acting as principal – and to the client if you are acting as his or her agent.

Lien

If you have carried out work on client documents and presented your bill, but the bill has not been paid, UK law gives you the right to retain possession of the documents until your fees have been paid. (This is called a 'particular lien' over the documents.)

You have a right of lien if:

- The documents belong to the client (not a third party)

student notes

- The documents have legitimately come into your possession (eg have not been obtained under false pretences) *and*

- You have worked on the documents and tendered a fee note – but the fees have not been paid in respect of that work (ie not past work).

You cannot exercise lien in relation to the statutory books and accounting records of companies, or where documents are claimed by an Administrator, Liquidator, Official Receiver or Trustee in Bankruptcy: they have a prior claim to the documents.

If in doubt, get more detailed advice from a solicitor or the AAT.

Retention of documents

As a general principle, the 'statute of limitations' means that once a certain amount of time has passed since a particular act or event, a legal action cannot be brought in relation to that act or event. Specific time limits apply for different matters (and in different legal systems), so you will need to get legal advice in detailed cases.

However, in the UK the time limit is six years for actions based on a simple contract or claim for civil damages. Six years is therefore the maximum time before which a disgruntled client could bring legal proceedings against the firm. Allowing another year to have it brought to court, **seven years** is probably the most sensible period to retain (and advise clients to retain) books, working papers and other documents.

Taxation records should be retained for **seven years**.

Signpost

See the *AAT Ethical Guidelines*:

- **Section 254**: Ownership of books and records
- **Section 255**: Lien
- **Section 256**: Retention of books, working papers and other documents

CHAPTER OVERVIEW

- Professional services must be promoted in such a way as to project an image consistent with the dignity of the profession and to maintain integrity in all actions and statements.

- Client acceptance procedures should take into account ethical principles including due care and independence, and also the need for due diligence under Money Laundering Regulations.

- You may not offer services which you are not properly authorised to undertake.

- A letter of engagement sets out all express terms in the relationship between you and your client in a particular assignment or engagement.

- Fees are normally calculated on an hourly or daily rate, but may also (cautiously) be estimated as an overall fee or offered on a contingency or percentage basis for appropriate assignments.

- When a client changes adviser, the prospective new adviser should carry out professional clearance procedures to obtain from the existing or previous adviser information relevant to the decision of whether or not to accept the appointment.

- Key principles in handling or holding clients' monies include: separation, dedicated use and accountability. In addition, it imposes higher risks of involvement in money laundering, and the need for appropriate investigations.

- Threats to objectivity and independence include: self interest, self review, familiarity, intimidation and advocacy threats. Safeguards may be legal, disciplinary and procedural.

- If you do something (or fail to do something) which results in financial loss to a person to whom you owe a duty of care, you may incur liability for professional negligence. Basic safeguards include: specification of responsibilities, warnings and disclaimers, and Professional Indemnity Insurance.

- The ownership of books and records depends on legal provisions, contract terms, the capacity in which you act for the client and the purpose of documents and records. You may retain possession of documents (exercise a right of lien) in pursuit of unpaid fees in relation to those documents.

- Documents should be retained for at least the period of limitation, during which a legal action may be brought.

KEY WORDS

A **letter of engagement** is written confirmation of the responsibilities of a provider of professional services and a client, in relation to a given assignment or engagement.

Lien is the legal right to retain possession of another party's documents or assets until their debt has been discharged.

Contingency or percentage fees are fees which are dependent on the results of the services provided.

Defamation is maliciously making an untrue statement which damages a person's reputation or standing.

HOW MUCH HAVE YOU LEARNED?

1   How long should books, working papers and other documents be retained?

2   What is 'lien' and when can it not be exercised?

3   What would constitute due diligence in gathering information about a prospective client, and why is it important?

4   If you enter into correspondence with the Revenue as tax agent of a client, to whom does this correspondence belong?

5   List the items to be included in a standard letter of engagement.

6   Explain the concept of 'separation' in regard to holding client monies.

7   You have been asked to draft guidelines for AAT student members on ethical advertising of professional services. Draft brief guidelines covering the content of advertisements.

8   You have been asked to prepare financial statements which rely on asset valuations previously prepared by your firm. What is the nature of the threat to your objectivity, here, and what safeguards may protect your objectivity in such a case?

9   Give one example each of potential (a) self-interest,

    (b) intimidation and

    (c) advocacy threats that may apply to a member in practice

10 A client has offered to engage you to perform a task which you have not previously dealt with, for that client, before. What is the nature of the threat here, and what safeguards might you put in place?

COURSE COMPANION ANSWERS

ANSWERS TO CHAPTER ACTIVITIES

Chapter 1: Ethical decision making

1   This is personal to you, so that you begin to think about your own assumptions and beliefs about what kinds of behaviour are 'OK' and 'not OK'. Some of these may be line with the ethical values of the AAT and accounting profession (such as being honest, telling the truth, being fair, working hard) and some may not be (such as using your work position for the benefit of family members, or offering gifts as a smoother of business relationships and negotiations). In a way, these instances – where your values differ from the professional standards – are more useful information: you know where your 'blind spots' are, and where you may have to modify your assumptions and habits.

2   There are many examples – and we will look specifically at them as we proceed through this Companion. Some basic ones you may have thought of include:

- Being accurate in recording your hours and expenses for your employer

- Not using your position for personal gain (eg by soliciting or accepting gifts or hospitality from clients or suppliers)

- Not offering unchecked, false or misleading information to clients (or in financial reports, statements or records)

- Not claiming to be a technical specialist in an area where you are not suitably qualified, skilled or experienced

- Obeying the law, as it applies to your work and personal conduct.

3   Examples include:

- Completing all study and assessments required to qualify, and applying them to the demands of your own organisation and work role (where applicable)

- Practising and getting feedback/checking on any areas of weakness

- Investigating opportunities for further learning and practice, to fill any learning gaps identified as a result of training or work demands (continuous learning)

- Staying up-to-date with new techniques, accounting standards, legislation etc, through reading and networking

- Learning how to use (proficiently) the procedures, equipment and software used by your employers

- Asking for help, guidance and information when you need it

4 This would be a breach of confidentiality. It could be damaging to the reputation of the client with the problems – and the information may be even more sensitive if the other client is a direct competitor! You may have 'authorisation' from your manager, but it is not legitimate: (S)he does not have the right to encourage you to breach your duty of confidentiality. (You may even consider that you have a responsibility to draw this to his or her attention.) It doesn't matter that the disclosure is potentially in the interests of the other client – since it so clearly damages the interests of the first one.

5 Examples include: health and safety at work; data protection (use of data held by organisations about individuals); equal opportunity and non-discrimination (including avoiding offensive and harassing behaviour towards others on grounds of sex, race and religious beliefs); and company law (eg on retention of documents). Plus – of course – not committing common law offences such as theft, fraud or assault!

6 Yes. This would be 'reckless' supply of information, which may be misleading or inaccurate (for all the client knows). The client simply has no way of knowing or guaranteeing that the information is true – which puts you in the position of supplying information which you are aware could be misleading or inaccurate to HM Revenue and Customs.

Chapter 2: Identifying ethical issues

1 The ability to identify fraudulent activities may be relevant if:

■ You have been asked to provide internal audit and/or financial control services to an organisation – in which case you need to know fraud when you see it!

■ You become aware of fraudulent actions in an organisation, or by a client – in which case you need to know what to do about it, and to whom to report it.

■ You are asked by an employer or client to be party to fraudulent actions – in which case you need to be aware of your obligation (and right) to refuse.

2 a) Reasons for overstating profits and/or net assets:

■ To ensure achievement on paper: may have to meet targets in order to secure a promotion; bonuses or remuneration may be linked to performance

■ Trying to conceal another form of fraud, such as theft

■ Need a healthy balance sheet to convince bank to give loan finance

■ Ailing company may be trying to entice equity investors

b) Reasons for understating profits and/or net assets:

■ To facilitate a private purchase of an asset from the business at less than market value

■ To defraud HM Revenue and Customs by reducing taxable profits or gains

■ Trying to force the share price down, so that shares can be bought below market value by friends or relatives.

3 a) Independence in appearance is the ability to demonstrate independence. The test is whether a reasonable person, in possession of all the relevant facts, would doubt whether you could be objective in the circumstances. This is important to protect the member's reputation – which may otherwise be in question despite actual objectivity (or independence of mind).

b) Examples of threats include: a financial interest in the outcome; a close personal or business interest in the outcome; reviewing or reporting on work in which you (or your firm) was involved; being threatened or bullied.

4 It would depend on a number of factors.

■ The value of the hospitality: a sporting event would not normally be regarded as significant – but it would depend on how lavish the package was (or how rare the tickets!). Would a reasonable observer think it likely to influence you?

■ The circumstances: in this case, the fact that the host is bidding for a major contract might suggest an attempt to influence the decision – but this would be irrelevant if, for example, you weren't the one with the authority to make the decision (but had a business contact at the firm).

5 a) Information which could be used against the interests of the organisation includes: details of its security procedures, legal dealings, new product plans (for use by competitors), or financial data.

b) Information which could be used against the interests of an individual includes: financial data, employment records, medical records and any personal data (as a potential breach of privacy).

6 You cannot disclose the client's difficulties to your friend. However, you could:

■ encourage him or her to exercise due diligence before accepting any contract – including a standard credit check (in which you would not be involved);

■ speak to your client about the ethical implications of entering into major supply contracts, given their financial difficulties.

7 Dishonest documentation would include a variety of the examples given for fraud, such as:

■ knowingly failing to record a payment where there is a requirement to do so;

■ knowingly preparing or using accounts which include false invoice or other records;

■ knowingly preparing or using an invoice which incorrectly describes a transaction, or the reason for a transaction.

8 Do not make any statement or promises in this regard, since you are not realistically in a position to do so.

9 Since you acted for the client in regard to the faulty return, you should:

■ Advise the client to inform HMRC.

■ If the client refuses, inform them in writing that you can no longer act for them.

■ Inform HMRC that you have ceased to act for the client, stating that you have received information indicating that the statements should not be relied upon.

Chapter 3: Personal and interpersonal skills

1   a)   Explaining CGT to a non-expert requires care in conveying information simply and clearly, and avoiding technical jargon (without patronising the client, however): find out what she knows and what she wishes/needs to know. You will also need to allow for the fact that English is not her first language. (If you are a male, you should also ensure that you behave ethically to her as a female: without prejudice or any form of harassment.)

       b)   The key communication issue in grievances is the need to preserve working relationships where possible. This is a colleague, so you should probably approach him, initially, to state your feelings about the criticisms and the impact that this behaviour has on your ability to work with him: an appropriately assertive approach – not blaming, and therefore likely to result in more constructive dialogue. If the behaviour does not alter, you may have to make a complaint to your joint supervisor: the communication issue here will be to convey relevant arguments clearly and calmly. (You might also wish to take notes of the conversations, if required for more formal grievance procedures.)

2   a)   'Dear [named individual]' closes with 'Yours sincerely'

       b)   The convention is 'Dear Sirs'

       c)   A copy reference is both a matter of co-ordination (avoiding the duplication of copying/transmission of messages) and of ethics (because it is only fair to let someone know who else is party to the information, particularly if it is a personal or sensitive matter).

       d)   A 'covering letter' (which informs the recipient about an enclosure) might be sent with all kinds of enclosures. Common enclosures include: payment cheques, invoices/statements, requested information (a report or brochure).

3   a)   Face to face discussion is good for challenging someone, because it allows for interactive questions and responses, so you can explore the matter in real time (and without the other person having time to prepare evasive responses). It allows you to observe non-verbal behaviour (which might help to determine whether someone is being open and honest – or not). It allows you to use non-verbal behaviour to impress on the other person how seriously you take the matter, and to use persuasion where appropriate.

           The disadvantage is that emotions may run high in conflict, without the 'cooling off' time/distance of more remote methods of communication. There may also need to be written confirmation of what was discussed, for later reference, as people's recall of discussion is not always complete or accurate.

       b)   Face to face discussion is good for negotiating contracts where the effect is to allow rapport to develop between the parties. It also allows for interactive questions and responses, to refine the detail of the terms.

           While verbal agreements can form contracts, detailed terms are better written down – for later/repeat reference, and evidence of what was agreed, in the event of any dispute.

4   Your role may include formal negotiations: negotiating your salary and other contract terms with an employer; negotiating fees and terms with clients; negotiating with suppliers to

provide you with goods and services; or perhaps an employee relations negotiation (if you are involved in a trade union or employee representative committee).

Your role may also include informal negotiations: persuading your supervisor for more time on an assignment; asking a colleague to 'cover for you' while you are on holiday; agreeing work allocations within a team and so on.

Negotiating the resolution of an ethical conflict may be formal (if it involves the grievance procedures of your employer or the AAT) or informal (if it involves your persuading another person to share your view).

5   a)   Your best option may be that your employer accepts your objections, and agrees to deal with the discrepancies in a proper manner.

Your worst option may be that your employer insists, despite all objections and measures that you take, to the point that you are forced to resign your position over the issue.

An acceptable, realistic or 'fall back' option (for this discussion) may be that your employer agrees to reconsider the matter, or get someone else to deal with the task. (This will not solve your problem in the long run, but may give you both time to consider your options.)

   b)   A win-win outcome might be where you uphold your ethical standards, but – in the course of discussion – you discover that the discrepancies can be positively resolved.

A win-lose outcome might be where you threaten to resign and your employer accepts: it will get someone else to conceal the discrepancies, and you will have to look for another job.

A lose-lose outcome might be where you back down and compromise your ethical standards – but are demotivated and uncommitted in your work.

   c)   You will need to practise assertive communication techniques and, if the employer is at all open, persuasive techniques, in addition to negotiation.

6   Health and safety law is not just important to HR professionals: you have an obligation to your employer to contribute to a safe and healthy working environment – and you should know your own rights, too.

You could update your knowledge in a wide variety of ways, depending on your situation, including:

■   Asking the HR or Health & Safety Officer in your workplace to explain the new provisions (and how they affect the firm's rules and procedures)

■   Looking up the latest provisions in back articles of your professional journal, or HR journals; doing a search on the Internet; looking up the rules and procedures in your office manual; calling the Health and Safety Executive to order their free booklets and updates.

■   Searching the Internet, relevant journals and/or adult education institutions for briefings or short courses on health and safety.

Chapter 4: Ethics for members in business

1   Several issues are raised by the carpet importers. There may be a genuine ethical issue in exploiting child workers – but we do not know how much this company pays and in what conditions the children work. The company believes it is benefiting communities.

However, the adverse publicity (though not about this company) may affect business, as consumers are highly sensitive to such issues. The company may wish to promote its ethical standards and objectives (benefiting communities, preserving a craft) more – and perhaps issue a 'Code of Ethics' in regard to its suppliers. It could take additional steps to reinvest in the communities (eg by funding a school or scholarships for children, or enforcing limits on hours worked by children, or paying higher wages).

The 'obvious' answer would be to stop importing child-made carpets – but if the company is right about this income benefiting communities, this would not be the most ethical approach.

2   An integrity-based approach would be more effective, as it helps people to be proactive about choosing to behave ethically; it makes ethical behaviour a positive (rather than a negative, trouble-avoidance) issue; it enables on-going development and problem-solving.

It would be less effective than a compliance-based approach, if the effect was to focus on 'values' – and neglect the letter of the law!

3   You should try to think about this yourself and come up with some ideas. A full answer is provided in the 'How it Works' section following the Activity.

4   Faithful service includes not accepting secret bribes or commissions and not disclosing confidential information.

5   Examples of employee dishonesty in a typical UK context would include:

- Being absent from work, pretending to be sick when you aren't. (You may not believe this is dishonest if you, or your workmates, are used to thinking of sick days as a form of informal 'extra holiday entitlement' – but it is defrauding your employer of time and money.)

- Blaming a colleague for mistakes you have made

- Sending personal e-mails (or making personal phone calls) on work time and systems (where this is not permitted)

- Falsifying time sheets or expenses lists (for reimbursement)

- Covering up for others who do any of the above.

6   A grievance procedure is a series of actions to be followed if an individual feels that (s)he has been wrongly or unfairly treated at work.

A formal grievance procedure is important so that:

a)   There is an avenue for complaints to be heard (rather than 'bottled up', which might escalate conflict in future)

b) Complaints are taken seriously, properly investigated and fairly dealt with, with the right of appeal to higher authority to ensure that this is so

7 This would be classified as money laundering. The guidelines on what to do about this are set out in law and regulations in the UK. In this case, you have a clear duty to 'blow the whistle' to the appropriate internal authority (the Money Laundering Reporting Officer) or the appropriate regulator (SOCA). This is a case where you should not take your suspicions to your supervisor or other managers initially, as this might be 'tipping off' under the regulations: it would give them the opportunity to conceal or destroy evidence, which might prejudice a later investigation.

Chapter 5: Ethics for members in practice

1 a) 'Largest' is at best ambiguous: it may refer to number of partners or employees, to the size or number of offices, or to annual turnover, for example.

b) The name of a practice might be misleading if it implies claims (such as being 'international' or specialising in a particular area) which cannot be justified. It may also be misleading if it could reasonably be confused with the name of another practice.

2 An individual may be verified by photo or other ID: a birth certificate, driver's licence and/or passport. A corporation may be verified by a certificate of incorporation, or a list of directors and shareholders, for example.

3 a) A disclaimer may be necessary so that the member is not responsible (and the client and third parties exercise due caution) for the consequences of use of the work by people, or for purposes, for which it was not intended.

b) It is the client's responsibility to provide full and accurate information: it should be clearly stated that the detection of irregularities and fraud rests with the client's management – and is outside the scope of the engagement.

4 It would be appropriate to offer services on a contingency basis in cases where the client's ability to pay (and therefore to access professional services) depends on funds gained as a result of the services: eg debt recovery, the sale of an asset, or a distribution of assets.

It would not be appropriate to offer financial reporting services on a contingency basis, because of the threat to objectivity.

5 a) Professional clearance protects the interests of the client, as it facilitates the exchange of information between previous and new advisers, which will help the latter to fulfil their responsibilities better.

Professional clearance protects the interests of the previous adviser, as it ensures that a client does not frivolously or fraudulently change advisers (without telling them), jeopardising their integrity or payment of their fees.

Professional clearance protects the interests of the new adviser, as it ensures that they are given the information required to make the decision of whether to accept the engagement or not (preventing them from taking on a client who will not pay fees, or who may get them involved in money laundering, for example).

b) The inference if a client does not want you to contact a previous adviser is that there is something (s)he does not want you to find out: (s)he has not paid the previous advisers' fees, for example (and may therefore be likely to do the same to you), or (s)he may be involved in fraudulent activity or money laundering (and is changing advisers to avoid detection).

6   A policy for managing client accounts in the best interests of the client would include elements such as:

- Ensuring that client accounts are separate from individual/practice accounts

- Ensuring that the bank acknowledges client ownership of monies in client accounts (protecting them from creditors, if the accountant goes bankrupt)

- Ensuring that monies are only drawn from the account on client instruction, or for client benefit (with strict accounting)

- Ensuring that the account never goes overdrawn (ie by withdrawing more than the account holds)

- Transferring monies to an interest-bearing account if a significant sum (more than £2,000) is likely to remain in the account for more than two months, and crediting interest to the client.

- Providing clients with statements of account, at least once a year.

7   If you are faced with an issue such as this in the assessment, the assessors will be interested in what matters you have considered – since there is not likely to be a 'right' conclusion to come to.

Matters to consider in relation to this situation include:

- The AAT's guidance: objectivity may be threatened, or appear to be, by undue dependence on any client.

- Despite high percentages for your office, each client represents less than 10% of the whole practice – unless other offices also undertake work for other branches of the same clients, in which case, the percentage will be higher.

- However, if each office in the firm runs independently (and profits are not shared through the national network), these clients may affect your office's independence.

- Are there safeguards in place? For example, does your office review the risk to its independence by its clients on a regular basis – or do partners from other offices review your office's work for these clients, as a check?

8   The final safeguard is refusal to accept or continue the assignment.

9   If unsure of your expertise, you should consult with an appropriate expert, or obtain guidance, to ensure that your knowledge is adequate and up-to-date. If still in doubt of your ability to fulfil your duty of due care, you should refuse to take on (or continue) the assignment, referring the client to other sources of help if appropriate.

This also raises the issue of CPD: you should make note of your shortcoming in this area, and take steps to access appropriate learning opportunities.

HOW MUCH HAVE YOU LEARNED? ANSWERS

Chapter 1 Ethical decision making

1   False. Group values are very important: eg in families and friendship groups (which is where we get our ideas from), national cultures and organisations (which establish ethical norms and expectations by which we have to operate).

2   The AAT needs to protect its reputation and standing, by maintaining standards of conduct and service among its members, in order to be able to:

a)   attract and retain members;

b)   enhance the reputation and standing of its members, so that they can attract and retain clients; and

c)   protect the reputation and standing of the profession, so that the public continues to put its trust in them.

3   Pressure or intimidation by a superior (or client)
A personal financial interest in the client's affairs, or the outcome of a decision
Personal or professional loyalty to one of the parties involved

4   This is an issue of technical competence and due care. As the client's tax adviser, you have a duty not to give information recklessly (eg pretending to know something when you really don't), especially if it might prejudice his interests. You would be at fault if you had claimed to be a tax specialist, and would normally be supposed to know the answer to this VAT question – and if you had failed to keep yourself up-to-date with reasonable technical requirements in this area. However, if it really was an obscure question (or if you had never claimed to be a specialist in this area, or if your contract with the client specifically excluded VAT matters), you would not (yet) have behaved unethically. You should clarify the limits of your expertise with the client, and seek information or guidance from the relevant source (a tax guide and/or specialist colleague).

5   You have a duty of confidentiality to the civil engineer, and this creates a genuinely tricky ethical conflict.

You should not disclose the information about the by-pass tender, even to help the petrol station client or café.

As part of your duty of care to the petrol station, you might want to advise them (in general terms) to monitor planning applications in the area – but this may not lie within the scope of your work for them, and if it had the effect of stirring up local protests that made the project fall through, you would have damaged the interests of your civil engineer client.

The fact that your sister is now an employee of the petrol station additionally raises an issue of objectivity: you will probably be unable to continue to act for them, because it might be supposed that you would act in their favour out of partiality – either in this instance, or in general.

You might similarly wish to give 'good news' to the café owners, to prevent them making a sale they would later regret. However, the pedestrian precinct plan is only a 'rumour': if you share this with them, your duty of care to them means that you cannot imply any certainty about the information.

You should not use the information in your own interests (eg to buy shares in the construction company. The civil engineer's comment was inappropriate.

6   The basic procedure is:

- Identify a potential threat to a fundamental ethical principle

- Evaluate the seriousness of the threat

- For any significant threat, apply safeguards to eliminate or reduce the threat to an acceptable level

- If safeguards cannot be applied, decline or discontinue the action or relationship giving rise to the threat.

Chapter 2: Identifying ethical issues

1   Examples include: theft of cash or stock; payroll fraud; teeming and lading; collusion with customers; collusion with suppliers; misuse of assets. (Details can be found in the chapter text.)

2   Cut-off dates allow the misrepresentation of financial statements. Sales can be deliberately over-invoiced (to increase turnover and profit): credit notes can be issued in the new financial year. Similarly, pre-year-end purchases not yet delivered can be held over for recording in the new financial year. A company which wanted to depress income/profits could, conversely, hold invoices over to the new financial year.

3   Shareholders, who may not get the returns they expect.

Suppliers may incur risk in extending credit without the security they expect

Management and employees may be frustrated by inaccurate information, or shortfalls in working capital.

4   It is illegal, under the Prevention of Corruption Act 1906.

5   Information may be confidential if it is:

- Shared with the explicit proviso or warning of confidentiality or restricted access

- Shared within a relationship of 'trust and confidence' under the law (including that between an accountant and a client)

- Protected by data protection and personal privacy law

- Subject to misuse against the interests of an organisation or individual.

6   You should tackle the client direct: you have not obtained the information in the course of work (and it is in the public domain), so you are free to use it as you see fit. In the interests of the client, you need to clear up the apparent omission, emphasising the need to record and declare all income.

If you have reason to believe that the previous year's tax return also omitted significant income, you should advise the client to inform the Revenue. If he refuses, you should inform him in writing that you must cease to act for him. You should also inform the Revenue that you have ceased to act for that client.

7   There is a clear threat to your independence in the case of reporting on payroll activities – when you have been involved in these yourself, within the period under review, and when the staff under review were until recently your nearest colleagues.

You should ensure that, if possible, you are not involved in the payroll area of the audit or that your work is checked by another auditor and that the reporting structure is such that you are not reporting directly to the payroll manager for whom you used to work (which may be perceived as a source of intimidation or influence).

Chapter 3: Personal and interpersonal skills

1   Active listening is where you enter into two-way dialogue with the speaker: asking questions, summarising, checking your understanding, giving helpful feedback and so on.

2   Ethical influencing methods involve giving the other person a genuine choice and good reasons to co-operate or agree with you: eg by logical argument, persuasion and bargaining/negotiating. Unethical influencing methods do not give the other person free choice: eg by deception, manipulation, intimidation or coercion.

3   There may appear to be an ethical issue of loyalty to your colleagues, or giving the manager a 'fair chance' to improve etc etc – but the only real ethical issue is a professional one: you have a duty of independence in providing internal audit services, and this means not being subject to coercion, persuasion or manipulation by a manager to alter the results of your audit.

An assertive (non-apologetic, non-aggressive) response would be: 'I appreciate that you are concerned about this, but it would be inappropriate and unprofessional of me to prejudice the results of the audit. That's how it is: please don't insist any further.'

4   a)

[Date… Time…]	
To:	jbenedetti@jaffordjolley.co.uk
From:	yname@jaffordjolley.co.uk
Cc:	
Subject:	Transatlantic Trading Ltd

James

I've just had a letter from a GJ Gillespie at a firm called 'X L Financial Services' in Guildford, stating that they have been engaged to provide investment advice to Transatlantic. They claim to have Transatlantic's authorisation to request all their financial records, books and statements.

Have you received any notification from Transatlantic to this effect? I assume that, in the absence of some express notification from them, confidential documents should not be released to a third party.

Your Name

b)

Jafford Jolley
Chartered Accountants
3 Southford Square
London SE2 2BX

G J Gillespie, Consultant
X L Financial Services
93 Hammond Terrace
Guildford
Surrey GU2 5LP

Your ref: GJG/13v0X

17 May 200X

Dear Mr or Ms Gillespie

Transatlantic Trading Limited

In reply to your letter of 13 May, requesting the records of the above client, I regret that we are unable to comply with your request without the express and direct authorisation of the client.

I am sure you understand that we have a professional obligation to protect the confidentiality of client information.

Please request Transatlantic Trading Limited to contact us in writing, stating that you have been engaged in this matter, and that they wish us to transfer the records to you.

Once we have received proper authorisation, we will endeavour to comply with your request as soon as possible.

Yours sincerely

Your Name

Accounting Technician

5   **REPORT**

> **To:**   The HR Manager
> **From:**   Your Name, Accounts Department
> **Date:**
> **Subject:**   Development planning using the Development Buddy Scheme

Identifying training/learning needs

Learning needs can be identified in a number of ways, including the following.

- Monitoring new developments in accounting (eg through professional journals and financial press) to identify newly emerging requirements, practices and techniques. Development Buddies (DBs) may exchange this information.

- Discussing job-related learning and improvement needs with the department head or immediate supervisor, or building on evaluations carried out as part of the formal appraisal scheme.

- DBs may observe and review one another's work and offer feedback on areas for improvement. Each may have an area of greater experience or knowledge to offer the other (eg if one is more senior, or the other has recently attended a study course).

Learning resources and opportunities

A wide range of resources is available, including:

- Formal learning opportunities: off-the-job courses or workshops, or systematic coaching and instruction on the job

- Self-learning resources: the Internet, books, journals and quality Press, for example. CD-, video- and Web-based tuition and assessment may also be available.

- Informal learning resources: getting feedback, advice, guidance and instruction from colleagues and professional networks.

- Experiential learning. One of the most effective methods of on-the-job learning is to undertake planned practice, reflect on the results (or get feedback) – and practise again: learning by 'trial and error'.

Evaluating and selecting learning methods

An effective learning method would be one which:

- Is suitable for the type of competence to be learned (eg giving hands-on practice where required)

- Takes into account the preferred learning style the trainee (eg if they prefer 'hands on' or theoretical learning)

- Takes into account the time available (eg if it can be combined with work demands) and the trainee's access to facilities (eg if it needs a computer or other equipment)

- Is cost-effective, in light of the benefits it is expected to bring the trainee and the organisation.

Chapter 4: Ethics for members in business

1   A bribe is a payment made to secure services to which a company is not legally entitled (eg bribing someone to disclose confidential information). Grease money is a payment made to speed up services to which the company is legally entitled, but which is being stalled or obstructed (eg offering money to process a development application more swiftly).

2   You are protected (Public Interest Disclosure Act) if:

- You disclose internally or to an appropriate regulatory authority (not necessarily if you make a public disclosure)

- You make the disclosure in good faith (not maliciously) and with reasonable grounds (not unfounded suspicions)

- You believe that the company has been, is, or is likely to be involved in a criminal offence, the endangerment of an individual's health or safety, damage to the environment – or the deliberate concealment of any of these.

3   The main responsibility lies with the company directors and the external auditors.

4   Openness, trust, integrity, respect, empowerment and accountability.

5   False: you owe your employer a duty of 'faithful service', which includes due care and skill. You should be honest about your limitations and ask for help.

6   **Guidelines: conflict of loyalty**

a)   As a professional, you have a dual loyalty to your employer and to your profession. In any conflict, the requirements of the law and your professional standards (both technical and ethical) take precedence.

Significant conflicts may arise if an officer of the firm asks you to:

- Break the law

- Break the rules and standards of your profession

- Put your name to, or otherwise be associated with, a statement which significantly misrepresents the facts

- Mislead or deceive the firm's auditors

b)   In such a case, the following procedure should be followed.

1)   Raise your concerns with your immediate superior where possible. Misunderstandings, differences of opinion and minor issues should be resolvable at this level.

2)   If the issue is significant, and unresolved (or if it concerns the immediate superior, in the first instance), the matter should be taken to a higher level of management and/or to the ethics committee for arbitration.

3)   You may wish to seek independent legal or professional advice (eg from the Professional Development or Ethics manager of your professional body) before proceeding further.

4) As with the general grievance procedures of the firm:

- All ethical complaints should be fully and fairly heard and investigated, without victimisation or threat of victimisation

- The complainant should have the right to be accompanied by a colleague or representative in any serious matter

- There should be the right of progressive appeal to higher levels until the matter is resolved

5) As a last resort, it may be necessary to inform management that if the conflict is not resolved, you will be forced to resign.

6) Prior to resigning, the professional should seek independent legal advice.

7) Accurate, dated records should be kept of all meetings, discussions and correspondence in relation to any of the above measures.

7 Select your examples from the Threats and Safeguards Checklist on page 71.

8 Recruitment criteria can be set to attract, and guide recruiters in selecting, staff members who value an ethical employer, and who have good track records, awareness and education/training in ethical principles.

Leadership can communicate ethical values, model ethical behaviour, express high expectations of ethical conduct in their staff/teams, and follow through on disciplinary action for unethical behaviour (or rewards and recognition for ethical behaviour). Leaders create the climate or culture in which ethics are (or are not) valued, and can (or cannot) be openly discussed.

Chapter 5: Ethics for members in practice

1 Books, working papers and other documents should be retained for at least the limitation period (beyond which they will not be required to defend a legal action). In UK law, this is generally 6-7 years: 8 years for taxation records.

2 'Lien' is the right to retain possession of documents or assets belonging to another party, until their debt has been discharged.

You can not exercise lien over documents if they belong to a third party; if they have not come legitimately into your possession; if the debt relates to past work (not related to those documents); if the documents in question are the statutory books and accounting records of a company; or if there is a claim on the documents by an administrator, liquidator, official receiver or trustee in bankruptcy.

3 Due diligence requires verification of the client's identity and certain 'Know Your Client' information (including its expected patterns of business, its business model and its source of funds). This is important to enable you to identify potentially suspicious transactions for the purposes of preventing (or disclosing) money laundering, under the Money Laundering Regulations 2003.

4   In this case, since you are an agent for the client (not a principal), the third party correspondence belongs to the client.

5   Items to be included in a standard letter of engagement include:

- The nature of the assignment

- The work to be undertaken (including any matters specifically excluded) and the format and scope of any reports to be delivered

- The start and end date of the assignment (if any), and the frequency with which it recurs (if relevant)

- The client's responsibilities (and limitations in the accountant's responsibilities where relevant: eg in submitting tax returns)

- The basis, frequency and rate of charges for services (including any contingency fees and expenses)

- Ownership of books and records created in the assignment

- Penalties for non-payment of fees

- Terms and disclaimers in relation to the use of the information by third parties or for purposes for which it was not intended

6   The concept of separation is that client monies should be kept in separate accounts from any monies belonging to the individual or firm providing the service. These may be general client accounts, or dedicated accounts for each client. The concept of separation should be notified to (and acknowledged by) the holding bank, in order to protect client funds from claims by creditors in the event that the accountant goes bankrupt.

7   **Guidelines on the content of advertisements for professional services**

As a member of the AAT, you are permitted to advertise – although as a student or affiliate member, you should not mention the AAT in the advertisements.

In general, advertisement content (like all promotional and other documents) must uphold the dignity of the profession, reflecting its high technical and ethical standards.

The AAT's Ethical Guidelines also state that:

- All advertisements (and other promotional materials) must comply with local law and Codes of Practice in relation to the honesty, truthfulness, clarity, decency and legality of their content.

- Any mention of fees in advertisements must not be misleading in detail (eg as to what is covered and how fees are calculated) and must allow a quality service to be offered to the client.

- All advertising claims must be objective and verifiable. Particular care must be given to claims of size or quality which may be misleading.

- Comparisons of service with those of competitors must be made with caution: they must be objective, verifiable and not misleading. It is not ethical to make disparaging references to, or comparisons with, the practice or services of other professionals.

8   The threat to your objectivity is one of 'self review'. This is regarded as a serious threat, particularly since it calls into question the independence of others whom you might otherwise ask to monitor your personal objectivity and conclusions: the firm prepared the valuations. In such a case, standard safeguards (such as professional standards and quality controls) would be insufficient.

It will help if the firm has mechanisms in place for the discussion and resolution of potential threats and conflicts. It may be necessary to involve, or consult with, independent third parties (eg non-executive directors or regulatory bodies, or in this case perhaps an independent valuation panel).

It may be possible to set up 'Chinese walls' and have the financial statements prepared by a unit of the firm that is completely separate and independent of the one which prepared the valuations. (An opinion on the adequacy of this should perhaps be sought from an independent adviser.)

If the threat cannot be eradicated, the firm may have to inform that client that it cannot act on their behalf in the matter of these financial statements.

9   Select your examples from the Threats and Safeguards Checklist at the beginning of chapter 5.

10   This is a potential threat to professional competence and due care. Safeguards include:

- Making sure you research the client's requirements thoroughly, before taking on the engagement

- Making sure that you have – or can develop or access – the required knowledge and competence

- Consulting an expert on the issues involved

- Ensuring that the letter of engagement manages the client's expectations and allows adequate time for competent performance.

REVISION COMPANION UNIT 32

chapter 1:
ETHICAL DECISION-MAKING

1   Define the following ethical principles:

    a)   Integrity
    b)   Objectivity
    c)   Professional competence and due care
    d)   Confidentiality
    e)   Professional behaviour

2   You have recently been helping a corporate client prepare a takeover for another company. The bid has been a success and the directors of your client are delighted to have acquired this other company at what they consider to be a very good price. In order to thank you for your help in this matter you and your husband have been offered an all expenses paid week in the company villa in Portugal.

    Should you accept this offer or not? Give your reasons.

3   You work for a firm of chartered accountants and are required to fill out a time sheet for each hour worked for each client each day. Last week you forgot to prepare the sheet for the week on Friday as normal and you are now doing it on Monday morning. However you are not absolutely sure how long you worked for each client on Thursday and Friday as due to pressure of work you did not record it.

    You have explained this to your manager who has told you not to worry about it and just put down something reasonable.

    What ethical issues does this situation raise?

4   While at a party at the weekend you meet a client of yours who is clearly very concerned about some VAT issues. You know enough about VAT to carry out your daily work but you are not an expert on the areas of imports and exports that your client is asking your opinion about.

    What ethical issues does this situation raise and what should you do about it?

5   As a member of the AAT, if you have any ethical concerns or dilemmas who at the AAT should you contact?

chapter 2:
IDENTIFYING ETHICAL ISSUES

1   What is meant by "independence in appearance"?

2   You have a retail client with a successful gift shop who recently opened up a second shop. You are aware that the client has taken on a full time sales person for the new shop but when checking the payroll records you can find no mention of this new employee or any payments to her.

    What should you do in this situation?

3   If you received a written report from your manager about concerns over the financial stability of one of your clients, which is marked "Confidential", would you be able to discuss the contents of this report with another accountant in your office?

4   You are a third year trainee accountant in the firm you work in and a second year trainee has just been taken on. You have been asked to look after the new recruit for the next few weeks until he understands how the job and the firm work.

    During one of your early conversations he tells you about his last firm and some of the clients that he worked for. He divulges information about the financial instability of a company that you know has approached your firm for some consultancy work.

    What ethical considerations does this situation raise?

5   Give three examples of different circumstances in which you are permitted to disclose confidential information.

chapter 3:
PERSONAL AND INTERPERSONAL SKILLS

1 a) If a letter is addressed "Dear Sir" how should you sign the letter off?

 b) What do the initials "Enc" at the end of a letter indicate?

2 What are the main elements of a report?

3 What is meant by assertiveness in communication with others?

4 Name five different types of learning resources or opportunities for Continuing Professional Development.

chapter 4:
ETHICS FOR MEMBERS IN BUSINESS

1   Give as many examples as you can of dishonest behaviour in the workplace which may however be acceptable in some organisations.

2   There are two basic approaches to managing ethics in organisations, the compliance based approach and the integrity-based approach. Briefly describe each of these approaches to managing ethics.

3   An employee has a fundamental general duty of faithful service to an employer. What does this mean?

4   What is meant by the term "whistle blowing"? What protection does a whistle blower have within the law?

5   In a limited company whose responsibility is it to detect and prevent fraud?

chapter 5:
ETHICS FOR MEMBERS IN PRACTICE

1 You work for a practising firm of chartered accountants who are reconsidering their advertising policy with the aim of gaining more clients. The following proposals regarding advertising have been made:

a) it should be stated that our fees are lower than most of our competitors
b) a free consultation should be offered to any prospective clients
c) it should be stated that we offer the best value for money amongst accountants in the area

For each of the advertising proposals, consider whether they are ethical and set out any concerns that you might have.

2 Explain the purpose of a letter of engagement and the main elements that should be included in the document.

3 A new client has approached your firm asking you to take on general responsibilities for preparation of year end financial statements and tax advice and returns. This client has been with her previous firm of accountants for some years.

What steps would you have to take before agreeing to act for this new client?

4 a) A client has asked you to hold a significant amount of money on his behalf pending the highly probable purchase by your client of another business.

Would you accept this money and if so how would you deal with it?

b) Another client has also asked you to hold a significant amount of money but has declined to tell you what the purpose of this money is.

Would you accept this money? Give your reasons.

5 You have just discovered that your brother-in-law has accepted a senior management position with a client of yours. What would be your reaction to this?

UNIT 32

AAT SPECIMEN SIMULATION

PROFESSIONAL ETHICS

COVERAGE OF PERFORMANCE CRITERIA

Element 32.1 Apply general principles and procedures for ethical compliance expected within the accounting sector

A   Identify and apply the fundamental principles of honesty and integrity

B   Highlight situations within professional work that require objectivity and fairness, and where judgements and actions could compromise personal or organisational integrity and reputation

C   Recognise the principles of effective Continuing Professional Development (CPD) to maintain professional and technical competence (to include sources of advice and information outside formal learning)

D   Recognise and explain why certain types of information should be regarded as confidential

E   Identify circumstances when it would be appropriate to disclose confidential information

F   Identify the key issues which ensure professional services are performed within the scope of professional ethics guidance

G   Make critical decisions to identify appropriate ethical behaviour when interacting with others in a variety of circumstances

H   Refer and seek advice from relevant sources for issues beyond own professional competence

I   Describe the types of contractual obligations you would have in providing services to clients, to include due care and carrying out assignments within a reasonable timescale

J   Discuss, agree and resolve any ethical conflict

Element 32.2 Develop, maintain and apply ethics in employer/employee situations

A   Describe the type of culture within organisations which supports and promotes high ethical values and helps resolve any conflict of loyalties

B   Resolve conflicting loyalties where an employer may ask you to perform tasks which are illegal, unethical or against the rules of standards of the accounting profession

C   Follow appropriate procedures where you believe an employer has committed or will commit an act which you believe to be illegal or unethical

D   Respond appropriately to requests to work outside the confines of your own professional experience and expertise

Element 32.3 Develop, maintain and apply ethics in public practice

A   Prepare appropriate letters of engagement and develop and implement a fair fees policy for your professional services

B   Identify and explain how specific situations can undermine professional independence.

C   Prepare a policy to be followed for handling clients' monies

D   Maintain independence and objectivity and impartiality in a range of circumstances

E   Make recommendations for a policy statement in relation to a client wishing to change accountant

F   Identify scope of professional liability

G   Prepare clear guidelines which should be followed to advertise your accounting services in a professional and ethical manner

H   Give advice to clients on retention of books, working papers and other documents

You are allowed 3 hours to complete your work.

Correcting fluid may be used but should be used in moderation. Errors should be crossed out neatly and clearly. You should write in black ink, not in pencil.

DATA AND TASKS

The situation

You are an accounting technician employed by a firm of chartered accountants based in a small town. You have responsibility for several clients, reporting to a partner who oversees your work, but you are the main contact for the clients.

Task 1

You have been asked to present a training session on professional ethics to some new trainees at your firm.

a)   Give a brief explanation of what is meant by each of the following.

-   Confidentiality
-   Integrity
-   Independence and objectivity
-   Professional and technical competence
-   Professional behaviour
-   Due care

b)   Read the 'client background information' and 'personal matters' sections (at the end of the tasks) and suggest how you can use these situations to demonstrate ethical issues that arise in every day practice, under the following headings.

-   Boat builders
-   Care Home
-   Art gallery
-   Your friend
-   Your brother in law
-   Your house

You should allow 40 minutes to complete this task.

Task 2

During your presentation one of the trainees makes the following comment.

'One of the reasons I wanted to get into accountancy was because I've heard you can get some really good deals from clients – I have a friend who even got a holiday because the client was so pleased with what he did for them.'

Set out your response to this remark.

You should allow 10 minutes to complete this task.

Task 3

Another trainee who is present at your presentation starts to tell everyone about the company where he previously worked. He explains how they used to pay people beneath the minimum wage, and how he had to pay people for a certain number of hours so that they would be entitled to state benefit, and made the rest up in cash. He also started to talk about the fact that the company didn't comply with regulations regarding the use of the machinery in the work place.

Suggest how you could use what he is saying to illustrate some ethical issues.

You should allow 10 minutes to complete this task.

Task 4

At the end of your training session it has been decided that you should include a session on claiming expenses and completing time sheets.

Explain why it is appropriate to include this in an ethics training session.

You should allow 10 minutes to complete this task.

Task 5

Having completed your training session you return to your desk to find a fax from a lending institution asking for financial information about one of your clients. The fax asks for an immediate response to enable the finance to be arranged as soon as possible. This is the first you have heard of this.

Identify the ethical issues which arise in this situation.

You should allow 10 minutes to complete this task.

Task 6

Your art gallery client has asked for some very specific advice on VAT issues. You know a bit about this, but have not dealt with it for 3 years and are not totally confident that you will give the right information. The client does not want to pay for this extra advice as they feel it should be part of the whole service.

Explain how you should deal with this situation and the issues that it raises.

You should allow 15 minutes to complete this task.

Task 7

In the evening you go to your local pub for a drink and, by chance, meet a client of the firm. He asks you several questions about inheritance tax and capital gains tax and then mentions that he has just come into quite a large sum of money and asks you to give him some advice on what would be the best thing to do with it.

Describe how you would respond to these questions, highlighting the ethical issues that come out of this.

You should allow 10 minutes to complete this task.

Task 8

a) You are conducting a meeting with a potential client.

Describe how you respond to the following questions:

   –   How much will you charge?

   –   How do I get the information from my previous accountant?

   –   A friend of mine said his accountant would not release any information once he changed accountants. Are they allowed to do that?

   –   I would like you to hold some money on my behalf for reasons that I would rather not discuss. Can you do this for me?

   –   The sign of a good accountant is the amount of tax they save you. How much tax do you think you will be able to save me?

b) Later in the day you receive a phone call from the potential client saying that he would like to change to your firm but he asks you not to write to his previous accountants. He says he will get all the information you require.

Explain what you should do in this situation.

You should allow 35 minutes to complete this task.

Task 9

You receive a phone call from an existing client asking you to prepare a funding proposal to assist in raising finance for their business. He says this is very urgent and would like you to start work on it straight away, but he asks that your fee be dependant on the success or otherwise in raising finance.

The client has specifically stated that it is only the proposal which he requires from you and will not need any further help with the raising of the money.

Identify the matters that need to be agreed before you commence work, including whether his suggestion regarding the fee is acceptable.

You should allow 10 minutes to complete this task.

Task 10

Your firm has decided to launch a new marketing campaign with the aim of increasing the number of clients and the fee income. The partners have asked for suggestions from all employees for ways of gaining new clients.

Some of the suggestions are set out below.

– Point out how much lower our fees are than the other local firms
– Point out that we give a better service than the other local firms
– Offer a 25% discount for the first year to all new clients
– Offer a commission to all staff for any clients introduced to the firm
– When new employees join the firm from another practice, give them an extra incentive to bring clients from their old firm with them
– Offer a free initial consultation for every potential client
– Offer commission to existing clients for any new clients they introduce

Comment briefly on the appropriateness of these suggestions, in relation to professional ethics.

You should allow 30 minutes to complete this task.

CLIENT BACKGROUND INFORMATION

Boat builders

This client is a limited company owned by a father and son. The company owns a property of relatively high value which was purchased three years ago and has since significantly increased in value. The property is now on the market as the company is struggling financially and needs to sell it quickly.

The son, who has the boat building expertise, wishes to leave to do other things. The father and son have fallen out over the exit route for the son and you are trying to mediate.

Over the years you have acted for them you have formed a good relationship with the son, but have always found the father difficult to talk to, and he shows little interest in or understanding of the financial aspects of the business. The son is planning to go into partnership in a new venture outside the area but he has said he would very much like you to continue to act for him. His ability to buy into the new venture depends a great deal on the settlement from the existing family business.

In passing you have heard the son say that he does not invoice for all jobs and puts the money straight into his personal account.

You have also been told that there is one employee who is not on the payroll and is paid in cash. He is particularly skillful and would be difficult to replace, and he will not work unless he is paid in this way.

Care Home

This is a care home for old people run by a married couple who happen to live in the same road as you do.

The maintenance of the road you live in is the joint responsibility of the residents. The road has recently been maintained, and you are all supposed to be sharing the cost, however, the owner of the care home arranged for the work to be done and you know that he had similar work carried out at the care home at the same time. You have asked him for a copy of the invoice for your own records, and although you have paid him, he keeps finding reasons not to show you the invoice. You therefore are beginning to suspect that the total cost will be put through as a business expense.

From looking at the books of the boat builders (above) you know that the husband has recently had a boat built. This is common knowledge, but his wife has told you that he has spent £1,000 on this, whereas you know from the boat builders' records that the boat cost £3,000.

This week you are preparing quarterly management accounts for the care home and you notice a 'boat builder' invoice in amongst repairs and maintenance which has been described as 'welding work': it is for £3,000.

The care home has a residential flat above it which the clients let out. When preparing their tax return, they say they have not let it out for the whole year, but there is something in the way they say it which makes you think this may not be true.

Property developer

You have a meeting arranged with a local property developer. He wants to discuss plans for future investments and he has asked you to bring along ideas for potential properties. He is always interested in getting a good deal and tends to let people hang on until they are desperate to sell.

He lets one of his properties out to another client of yours who runs an art gallery (details below). The developer has told you that he plans to sell very soon.

Art gallery

Your clients have been talking about their long term plans for their gallery and how their present location is ideally suited to their plans. They are thinking about investing a large amount of money in changing the premises to the way they need it for their business and are currently spending a lot of time on planning this at the expense of their existing business.

A personal friend of yours exhibits at the gallery and is paid a commission for any sales made. From the work you have done on the accounts it appears that the gallery has been taking prints of your friend's pictures and selling them without her knowledge.

PERSONAL MATTERS

Your friend

Your friend also has a gallery in the town and she has told you that she is 'letting' some space to a client of yours who is a VAT-registered sole trader. Your friend says he is trying to break into the art world and has been quite successful in selling some of his paintings. His accounts, which you prepare quarterly, show no income from this source.

Your brother in law

Your brother in law has recently been offered a job with one of your larger clients. He and your sister are very excited and see it as a major career move; the additional money he will be earning will enable them to start a family and buy a larger house.

You were aware that your client was looking to recruit, but the level of pay that your brother in law has been told is far higher than the figure you had been given by your client.

The last set of accounts you prepared for the company were qualified on a going concern basis and you know the company has serious financial difficulties.

Your house

You are having an extension built by a local builder who is not a client. This is completely outside your professional work. He offers to do the build for cash so that you don't have to pay VAT.

REVISION COMPANION UNIT 32

answers

answers to chapter 1:
ETHICAL DECISION-MAKING

1 a) **Integrity** can be described as honesty, fair dealing and truthfulness in all professional, business and personal financial relationships.

   b) **Objectivity** – this is based on the idea that all professional judgement should be made fairly on the basis of objective and intellectually honest appraisal of information, free from prejudice, bias and partiality and free from factors that might affect impartiality.

   c) **Professional competence** is based upon the fact that clients and employers are entitled to competent professional services based upon up-to-date technical and ethical standards. Therefore individuals should not accept or continue an assignment which they are not competent to perform and they should maintain and develop their professional and technical competence. **Due care** is a legal concept which states that having accepted an assignment an individual has a contractual obligation to carry it out to the best of their ability, in the clients' best interests and within reasonable time scales.

   d) Confidentiality of information means that you should not use or disclose information unless you have specific and proper authorisation from your client or employer or you are legally or professionally entitled or obliged to disclose it.

   e) Professional behaviour means behaving in a way that maintains or enhances the reputation of your profession.

2 This offer of a free holiday should not be accepted due to the principles of professional independence and objectivity. The offer is of significant value over and above what the client has paid for your advice in the matter of the takeover. Such a gift, if accepted, could be viewed from an observer's point of view as payment in kind for special favours or may indicate that you may be biased towards that client in future.

3 From a personal point of view this is a matter of integrity. Your clients are charged fees on the basis of the hours that you and other members of the firm work for them, so it is important that the recording of these hours is accurate. Therefore you are right to be concerned about not knowing the precise hours and should ensure that this situation does not happen again.

   Your manager's attitude of "don't worry" raises concerns about the firm's attitude to ethical considerations. If there is a top down approach that does not worry about minor ethical matters then this will have an effect on all employees and may also encroach when more important ethical matters are under consideration.

4   This raises issues of due care and professional competence. You know that you do not have the knowledge to answer these questions at this time and in this situation. For your own professional safety you should make the client clearly aware of this and not be prepared to give any opinion as this may be relied upon by the client despite the circumstances. The most appropriate form of action would be to make an appointment with the client to discuss the matter properly after you have done some research into these specific areas.

5   The AAT's Director of Professional Development

answers to chapter 2:
IDENTIFYING ETHICAL ISSUES

1   "Independence in appearance" is the concept of being seen to be independent. This is about the ability to demonstrate independence by avoiding situations which would cause a reasonable and informed observer to question your ability to be objective.

2   In this situation you will probably be suspicious that the employee is being paid in cash in order to avoid the tax consequences of employment. You need to ensure that your suspicions have some validity but you must be aware of the dangers of "tipping off" your client. Payroll fraud is an offence which is reportable to SOCA.

   Your first step is probably to speak to your manager about your concerns and it may then be suggested to you that you speak to your client in general terms about the seriousness of accurate and truthful reporting. If there is no change in the payroll situation after this then you should report the situation to your firm's Money Laundering Reporting Officer if you have one, or to the senior partner if not.

3   If any information that you receive is officially classified as "Confidential" then you should only discuss this information with the person who sent it to you.

4   The new recruit is acting unethically by passing on confidential information to you. You should therefore have a discreet word with the recruit to explain the ethical issues involved. The fact that he has given you confidential information about a company that your firm may provide consultancy services to is also confidential information which ethically you cannot pass on to others in your firm. However it may be possible, tactfully and in general terms, to suggest to the manager dealing with this potential client that their financial stability is considered.

5   a)   When the client or employee has given proper authorisation to disclose the information.

   b)   When it is necessary to disclose information in order to perform your work properly or according to technical standards and ethical requirements of your profession.

   c)   You are required to disclose the information by law.

answers to chapter 3:
PERSONAL AND INTERPERSONAL SKILLS

1 a) Yours faithfully

b) Something is enclosed with the letter.

2 The main elements of a report are:

- name of person preparing it
- name of person/persons it is to
- subject
- date
- executive summary
- introduction
- findings
- summary
- appendices (not always required)

3 Assertiveness involves standing up for your own rights or beliefs, but in such a way that you do not violate the rights of the person you are communicating with.

4
- courses, workshops, seminars
- books, newspapers, professional journals, technical publications
- computer packages, CD-ROMS
- Internet sites
- internal manuals
- colleagues, superiors at work

Note that only five were required.

answers to chapter 4:
ETHICS FOR MEMBERS IN BUSINESS

1   Examples of dishonest behaviour in the workplace that may be acceptable in some organisations include:

- making personal telephone calls during working hours
- making personal use of the internet within working hours
- inflating expense claims
- inflating overtime hours
- using office stationery for personal use
- taking "sick days" when not really ill

2   A compliance based approach to managing ethics is mainly designed to ensure that the company acts within the letter of the law so that violations are prevented, detected and punished.

An integrity based approach combines a concern for the law with an emphasis on personal responsibility and decision-making in ethical behaviour. It encourages people to develop strong ethical standards and values and is evidenced by ethics being part of the organisation culture.

3   An employee's general duty of faithful service to an employer is:

- to give a fair day's work for a fair day's pay
- to obey lawful and reasonable orders and instructions
- to use skill and care to protect the interests of the employer

4   Whistle blowing is the disclosure by an employee of illegal or unethical practices by the employee's employer.

Under the Public Interest Disclosure Act 1998 in the UK there is some protection for a whistle blower. The employee cannot be dismissed for disclosing otherwise confidential information internally or to an appropriate regulator, if they do so in good faith and have reasonable grounds to believe:

- that a criminal offence has been, is being or is likely to be committed

- that the health and safety of any individual has been, is being or is likely to be endangered

- that the environment has been, is being or is likely to be damaged

- that information on any of the above has been, is being or is likely to be deliberately concealed.

5   In a limited company it is the responsibility of the directors to prevent and detect fraud.

answers to chapter 5:
ETHICS FOR MEMBERS IN PRACTICE

1   a)   Firstly if fees are mentioned it must be made clear what is covered and how the fees are calculated. You must also ensure that if the low fees are being used as a promotional tool that you can actually provide a quality service at that price.

           It must also be possible for you to demonstrate that your fees are in fact lower and are comparable to those of other accountants.

    b)   It is perfectly ethical to offer prospective clients an initial free consultation.

    c)   Such a claim is subjective and difficult to prove and therefore should not be used in any advertising material. Any such comparisons should be objective, factual, verifiable and relating to the same services.

2   A letter of engagement provides written confirmation of the agreement with the client as to the nature and scope of the work to be undertaken and the responsibilities of both the client and the accountant in the relationship.

    The main elements of a letter of engagement are:

- the nature of the assignment, the work to be undertaken and the report to be delivered

- the start date, length of assignment, whether it is a recurring assignment and whether the engagement is open-ended

- the client's responsibilities

- the basis, frequency and rate of charging fees, treatment of expenses and billing arrangements

- ownership of books and records created in the assignment

- penalties for non-payment of fees

- whether the client can share the work with third parties or use it for other purposes

- disclaimer of liability for other uses.

3   When approached by a new prospective client the following steps should be taken:

- explain to the prospective client that your professional duties require you to communicate with the existing accountant and get the client's permission for this

- request the client to notify the existing accountant of the proposed change and to authorise them to co-operate with you as a possible successor

- ■ write to the existing accountant asking for any issue or circumstance which might be relevant to your decision as to whether or not to accept the new appointment

- ■ if no reply is received write again stating your intention to accept the appointment unless a reply is received within a reasonable and specified time

- ■ decide whether to accept the appointment based upon the circumstances and any issues that you have been advised of

- ■ draw up and submit an engagement letter

- ■ request from the previous accountant any books and papers which belong to the client.

4   a)   This would appear to be a valid purpose for you to hold the money therefore it would be accepted. The procedure would be as follows:

- ■ a separate bank account should be maintained for the monies (although this could be a general client account rather than a specific account for this client provided that it is separate from the firm's bank account)

- ■ monies should be promptly deposited and only drawn from the account on the client's instruction or for the benefit of the client.

- ■ the client account should never be overdrawn and if there is more than £2,000 likely to remain in the account for more than two months then the money should be placed in a separate interest bearing account with all interest being credited to the client.

- ■ accurate and up-to-date records of the amount in the account must be kept and statements should be provided to the client at least once a year

b)   In this case you cannot accept the monies as you cannot hold client's monies without verifying the commercial purpose of the transaction and the source and destination of the funds.

5   The fact that your brother-in-law is working for your client is a threat to your objectivity. You should disclose the personal interest to your manager and in turn this will probably be disclosed to the client.

AAT SPECIMEN SIMULATION

UNIT 32

ANSWERS

Task 1

a) | Principle | Explanation |
|---|---|
| Confidentiality | Members need to respect the confidentiality of information obtained (from employers and clients) in the course of professional work. |

This means not using the information and not disclosing the information to others, unless:

- The client or employer has given specific and proper authorisation or

- There is a legal or professional entitlement or duty to disclose the information.Note that confidentiality is also an important value in personal working relationships, as the basis for trust.

Integrity	Members are required to uphold honesty, fair dealing and truthfulness in all professional, business and personal financial relationships.
Independence and objectivity	All professional judgements should be made fairly:

- On the basis of objective and intellectually honest appraisal of information

- Free from all forms of prejudice, bias and partiality

- Without allowing other factors or influences to compromise or override objectivity

Professional and technical competence	Clients and employers are entitled to competent professional service based on up-to-date technical and ethical standards.

This means that:

- Members should not accept or continue an assignment which they lack the competence to carry out to a satisfactory standard, unless they are able to access the guidance or assistance required.

- Members have an on-going duty to maintain and develop their professional and technical competence, to keep pace with developments in the techniques, practice, legislation and regulatory guidance relevant to their work.

Professional behaviour	Members should behave in a way that maintains or enhances the reputation of the profession: bringing credit, not discredit.This involves basic values such as professional courtesy and consideration – as well as reflecting the 'dignity' of the profession: its high technical and ethical standards.
Due care	Due care is a legal concept which states that, having accepted an assignment, you have a contractual obligation to carry it out to the

best of your ability: in the client's best interests, within reasonable timescales (given the scope and nature of the assignment) and with proper regard for the technical standards of the profession.

b) For confidentiality reasons, some aspects of the case studies should perhaps not be used in the training presentation, but I have noted the principles that they illustrate.

Boat builders

The assignment to mediate between the father and son can be used to illustrate a **conflict of interests**: a gain for one client might mean a loss for the other.

In this case my closer relationship with the son might be perceived as a **threat to objectivity** arising from 'familiarity'. In addition, there is an inducement for me to get a better settlement for the son, in the form of the offer of future work (and fee income) arising from his new venture: this is a 'self interest' threat, and as such, might be considered unsurmountable by routine safeguards. It would therefore be advisable for another member of the firm to undertake the mediation: the independence of the firm would then be beyond question (preserving 'independence in appearance').

More seriously, the son has disclosed his personal involvement in fraud (by theft of un-invoiced payments) and the firm's involvement in payroll **fraud** (by improper payment of the employee). These are both reportable to the Money Laundering Reporting Officer of our firm (or the NCIS). Without 'tipping off' the client, under the Money Laundering Regulations, I will need to confirm the facts (with the son) and advise both clients of the seriousness of accurate reporting (particularly in valuing the business for a potential buyer).

I will discuss the matter with my supervising partner before taking any action: the firm may decide that it cannot continue to act for a client that is known to be dishonest.

A side issue concerns **confidentiality**. I know that the boat builders are keen to sell their property – and I know that the property develop client is looking for property. It would be unethical to disclose the boat builder's situation to the property developer, however it may be possible to benefit both clients by:

■ Asking the property developer for permission to disclose his interest and name to potential vendors.

■ Telling the boat builders about the developer – and introducing them if appropriate. (If the firm gets any kind of reward for this, it must be clearly disclosed to both parties.)

■ Advising both clients, in writing, to get independent professional advice regarding the sale/purchase of the property (so that the firm has no conflict of interest in the outcome).

Care Home

This scenario illustrates the handling of **suspicions** – rather than evidence of fraud.

It would be a falsification of financial statements to put through as business expenses the total cost of the road maintenance (although the cost has been shared) and the personal expenses on the boat (which appear to have been deliberately described in a misleading way). It would likewise be fraudulent to fail to record the rental income on the tax return. However, I have no evidence to support my suspicions.

I will cover the firm by asking the owners for a general written assurance that only business expenses are included in the accounts, and that all income has been disclosed in the tax return. I will also ensure that, when the accounts are prepared, the invoices for road maintenance and 'welding' are investigated – and, if my suspicions turn out to be correct, appropriately dealt with in the care home's accounts.

The apparent lie by the husband to his wife, as to the true cost of the boat, is not relevant to my professional work: I have no duty or entitlement to use the information.

Art gallery

This scenario can be used to illustrate **confidentiality**. I cannot tell the art gallery owners that the property developer is planning to sell the gallery property. However, I can protect the interests of the art gallery clients by:

- Encouraging the property developer to be socially responsible by letting tenants know as early as possible of his plans to sell

- Advising the gallery, in general terms, to check their security of tenure and the term remaining on their lease, before making long term plans.

More seriously, the gallery appears to be **illegally** defrauding your artist friend of commission, by selling prints without her knowledge. Again, without 'tipping off' the client, I will advise them of the need to comply with copyright law and persuade them to correct the situation. If they refuse, I will have to report them (having discussed the matter with my partner) to the MLRO of the firm. I am not entitled to report them to my artist friend, as this would be a breach of confidentiality.

Your friend

This illustrates the use of information not acquired in the course of professional work.

The friend's art gallery is in the public domain, so the fact that my client is selling paintings there is not covered by confidentiality: I can tackle him directly about the discrepancy in his declared income.

Your brother in law

This is another illustration of **confidentiality** and **objectivity**.

I cannot disclose information about the client to my brother-in-law, but (considering general consequences and obligations) it would be ethical to protect him and the family by:

- Suggesting that he undertake 'due diligence' by looking at the accounts and audit report (which are on public record) before accepting the job

- Discussing with the client the ethicality of continuing to recruit while they are in financial difficulties.

If my brother-in-law accepts the appointment, there may be a perceived threat to my objectivity. I will disclose the family relationship to my firm – which will then have the obligation to disclose it to the client.

Your house

This is an issue of integrity. It would be inappropriate for me to accept the builder's offer, as my personal integrity should be beyond reproach. However, the matter did not arise in the course of my professional work, so I have no responsibility to report it.

Task 2

I will have to inform the trainee – and the group – that he has been misguided in his expectations. Accountancy is not a field in which gifts are often received. Indeed there is a duty (under the principle of objectivity, and in some circumstances, anti-corruption law) to decline any significant gifts – such as a holiday.

A gift should not be (or be perceived by a reasonable and informed observer to be) a threat to objectivity: this generally rules out accepting gifts other than 'token' offerings such as a calendar or bottle of wine at Christmas.

There is a further ethical issue in the assumption that 'extra' financial recompense is required: a client should get quality service in return for the agreed fee.

Task 3

There are two major ethical issues here.

- The trainee owes a **duty of confidentiality** (as part of his duty of 'faithful service') to his employer – even after he has left the company. He should not be sharing detailed information about its dealings – particularly where they are damaging to its reputation.

- There is a **conflict of loyalty**. Once the employee became aware that his employers were committing illegal acts which could compromise his professional integrity, his first duty was to persuade the employer to cease the illegal activity and put things right. If they refused, having sought advice from a legal adviser or the AAT's Director of Professional Development (if he is a member), he may have had to take further action, including resignation.

Threats to health and safety must be disclosed both internally (to a Health and Safety officer) and to appropriate authorities (the Health and Safety Executive): the 'whistleblower' in such a case is protected by the Public Interest Disclosure Act in the UK.

Task 4

Claiming expenses and completing time sheets is relevant to professional ethics because they reflect on members' **integrity**.

Values in regard to honesty are part of organisation culture, and it may be that there is a lax attitude to such matters, communicated by the partners and HR systems of the firm. It may be 'common practice' to inflate expenses claims, but this means taking money to which you are not entitled: it amounts to fraud. Similarly, it may be seen as a waste of time accurately to record time spent on assignments, but inaccuracy may result in hours being charged to the wrong client.

The fact that these matters are included in induction training suggests that this firm takes the matter seriously, and sets high standards of honesty as a cultural norm. This should be reinforced by consistent modelling by the partners, and by other HR systems such as disciplinary procedures, appraisal and reward.

Task 5

My first obligation is to protect the **confidentiality** of the client's data. I will confirm with the client that the request is genuine, and that I have her authority to disclose the information to this lending institution.

I will send the requested information by letter (if time permits) rather than fax, so that I can protect confidentiality. The letter will be clearly marked: 'Confidential'.

In order to protect the firm from **liability** arising from the lending institution's reliance on the information, it will also include a disclaimer to the effect that:

- The information is given for this user and purpose only, and should not be relied on by third parties or for other purposes

- It has been prepared from information, records and explanations provided by the client, without carrying out an audit

- The firm takes no financial responsibility for the information.

Task 6

It is my responsibility to give the client correct advice, as part of my duty of care.

Since I am not sure that I have accurate or up-to-date information about these specific VAT issues, I must:

- Take steps to consult with a VAT expert within the firm, to ensure that my advice is appropriate

- Get legal advice about liability, if the consequences of the advice turning out to be incorrect (although given in good faith) are particularly heavy.

- Consider whether knowledge in this area is likely to be required again in my work: if so, I have a responsibility to ensure that I am up-to-date with technical and regulatory requirements. I could consult with the VAT experts in the firm, use the firm's library of legislation and text books, or refer to the VAT web site.

An additional issue is raised by the fact that the client does not want to pay extra for this advice. If an overall fee has been agreed, and the terms of the letter of engagement are sufficiently open to include the task, it would not be inappropriate to include it. However, I will have to ensure that the agreed fee is sufficient to allow me to perform the additional task (and future work within the terms of engagement) at the expected level of quality – without having to 'cut corners'. The terms of engagement may have to be altered to accommodate the new task (eg if VAT calculations were specifically excluded from the original assignment).

Task 7

First of all, I would need to consider whether I have the competence to answer the questions about inheritance tax and CGT.

If not, I would have to tell the client openly that I did not know the answers, would rather not give an 'informal' answer on the basis of insufficient information, and would undertake some research. Even if I felt competent to answer the questions, and was drawn into discussion, I would make clear that any advice I gave was only informal, and based on incomplete information: consideration in detail might cause me to revise my advice.

The preferred option would be to put the situation on a more professional footing, with agreed terms of engagement and a fuller discussion – which would protect both parties. I would encourage the client to make an appointment to discuss the matter properly.

There is a particular issue involved in giving advice on how the client could use the inheritance: this may constitute investment advice – and I would not be allowed to give it, unless I was authorised by the appropriate regulatory regime. (If I was subsequently engaged by the client, the terms of engagement should explicitly exclude investment advice – or state the regime by which I was authorised to give it.)

Task 8

a)

Client's question/comment	Response
How much will you charge?	I explain that fees are charged on the basis of the time spent (as an hourly or daily rate) and work involved. This ensures that the fee is sufficient to enable quality work to be performed.
	I may be able to quote an estimated fee, if the tasks are routine (and I have authority to do so). If there is a risk that the amount may be substantially higher, I will state this clearly to the client.
	In appropriate circumstances, the fee may be contingent on results.
How do I get the information from my previous accountant?	I explain that the client informs the previous accountant that he has asked us to act for him. I then contact the previous accountant (in a 'professional clearance letter') to ask whether there are any professional reasons why we should not act for him. All being well, and a letter of engagement exchanged, I ask the previous accountants to hand over the client's information.
A friend of mine said his accountant would not release any information once he changed accountants.	I explain that this should not happen: an accountant should release information when requested by a successor. The only circumstances in which this might not happen is if the accountant exercises a right of 'lien': a right to hold onto documents belonging to the client until the client has paid the fees relating to the work performed on them.

I would like you to hold some money on my behalf for reasons that I would rather not discuss.	I explain that under professional guidelines, I need to know the purpose of the transaction, and the source and destination of the funds. If the client refuses to tell me, I will have to decline to hold the monies, as there is a risk of involvement in money laundering (handling funds arising from, or to be used for, criminal activity).
The sign of a good accountant is the amount of tax they save you.	How much tax do you think you will be able to save me? I explain to the client that an accountant provides a range of services that offer added value: not just tax saving. I also explain that I cannot make any promise or suggestion as to amounts of tax that can be saved: tax returns are always open to challenge.

b) The client's refusal to let you contact the previous accountant directly – in the face of my clear explanation of the professional guidelines to this effect – is suspicious. It looks as if the client is aware of reasons why I should not accept the appointment, which would come to light in the course of professional clearance: he may be in dispute with the previous accountant over non-payment of fees, or he may be concerned about what the previous accountant will disclose.

I will emphasise that, under my professional guidelines, I need to obtain professional clearance before I can act for him. If he does not agree, he may withdraw – or I may have to suggest that he seeks another adviser.

Task 9

This task is likely to be separate to any existing terms of engagement, and as such should be set out in a separate letter of engagement, following the agreement of terms.

The letter of engagement should include:

- The nature and scope of the assignment: to include the preparation of a funding proposal, but not further help with raising the finance (excluding investment business, as regulated by the Financial Services Act)

- The format of the funding proposal report to be produced

- The start and completion (report submission) dates, and the fact that the engagement is non-recurring

- The client's responsibilities: providing full and accurate information for the preparation of the proposal; responsibility for any actions or decisions taken on the basis of the information

- The basis, frequency and rate of charge for the service. (In this case, it would not be inappropriate to charge a contingency fee, as an agreed percentage of the finance raised.)

- Ownership: the report given to the client to be the property of the client, but all working papers to belong to the firm

- Third parties: use of the report solely for raising finance from a specified third party, and not to be used for any other purpose. (A disclaimer may be included, to the effect that the firm is not liable for losses resulting from reliance on the report by unspecified third parties or for other purposes.)

Task 10

Suggestion	Comment
Point out how much lower our fees are than the other local firms	Caution is required in making any promotional comparisons between one firm's practice, services or fees and those of others. Any such comparisons must be objective, verifiable and not misleading (eg relating to the same services).
	In addition, the offer of low fees must be consistent with maintaining service quality – and with the dignity of the profession.
Point out that we give a better service than the other local firms	Again, caution is required in making promotional comparisons. This statement may be unethical if it discredits or denigrates other firms or their service. It may also be difficult to verify, as quality of service is a vague concept.
Offer a 25% discount for the first year to all new clients	It is not inappropriate to 'discount' fees, as long as the quality of the firm's work will not suffer as a result.
	The key issue is to clarify what is being discounted, in order not to confuse or mislead clients. The discounted fee should clearly represent a 25% reduction on the fee that would have been charged by this firm for the same service.
Offer a commission to all staff for any clients introduced to the firm	This is not inappropriate as a promotional strategy, although care may be taken in regard to new staff (as discussed below).
When new employees join the firm from another practice, give them an extra incentive to bring clients from their old firm with them	Professional judgement and integrity should be exercised by new staff 'bringing clients with them' from previous employers, however: bad will may result from such a practice.
Offer a free initial consultation for every potential client	This is appropriate as a method of discussing fees and terms. (There might be an issue if advice was given at such a consultation, however, given that terms had not been agreed.)
Offer commission to existing clients for any new clients they introduce	If a commission, fee or reward is offered to a third party (other than employees) to introduce a client, the firm must ensure that:

- The new client is aware of the arrangement with the third party

- The third party accepts responsibility for carrying out the introduction in accordance with ethical standards comparable to those of the AAT (whether as a member of a body or in compliance with similar standards).

INDEX

AAT's Director of Professional Development 13
AAT's Guidelines on Professional Ethics 4
AAT's Guidelines on Professional Ethics 32
Accountability 67
Advertisements 89
Advertising claims 90
Advertising standards 89
Advocacy 72, 88, 106
Advocacy threats 15
Anti-corruption legislation 30
Anti-Terrorism, Crime and Security legislation 31
Assertive communication 46, 54
Assertiveness 54, 59

Bad debts 26
Body language 53
Business ethics 64

Changes in appointment 99
Client acceptance procedures 92
Collusion with customers 26
Collusion with suppliers 26
Commission 91
Communication 46
Competence 6, 9, 72
Competitor comparisons 90
Compliance-based approach 65
Conceptual framework 14
Confidentiality 7, 9, 20, 32
Conflict of interests 107
Conflicting loyalties 77
Contingency fees 97
Continuing Professional Development (CPD) 56
Contract 38, 43
Contract for services 38, 94
Contract of service 38
Contracting to supply services 93
Contractual obligations 38
Criminal Justice Act 1993 36

Critical decision-making on ethical issues 11

Defamation 113
Discussion 53
Disparaging statements 90
Due care 7, 9, 20
Duty of care 109

Employment contract 69
Empowerment 67
Error 41
Ethical conflict 17
Ethical guidelines 11
Ethical organisation 64
Ethical principles 5
Ethical reporting 40
Ethics 4, 20
Ethics and the law 11
Expenses 97
External auditor 81

Face to face verbal communication 47
Fairness and respect 76
Faithful service 69
Familiarity 71, 88, 105
Familiarity threats 15
Fees 90
Fees policy 97
Fictitious sales 26
Financial interests 73
Finding clients 90
FRAUD 25, 43, 81
Fundamental principles 5

Gifts 29
Grievances 18
Guidelines 40

Handling clients' money 103
Harassment 90
Health and safety 76
Honesty 75

Hospitality 29

Illegal or unethical conduct by an employer 79
Independence 28, 42, 104
Independent legal advice 12
Inducements 73
Influencing 48
Informing 48
Integrity 5, 9, 67
Integrity-based (or principled) approach 65
Intentional misrepresentation 25
Internal audit 42
Interpersonal skills 46, 59
Intimidation 71, 88, 105
Intimidation threats 15

Know your client (KYC) information 92

Law 4
Letter heading 90
Letter of engagement 94, 113
Letters 50
Lien 111, 113

Managing ethics 65
Manipulating year-end 26
Members in practice 87
Misrepresentation of the financial position 28
Misuse of assets 26
Money laundering 35, 43, 93, 100
Money Laundering Regulations 2003 36
Money Laundering Regulations 2007 92
Money Laundering Reporting Officer 36

Negotiation 53, 54, 59

Objectivity 6, 10, 20, 28
Omission 41
Openness 67
Organisation culture 4, 20, 67
Over-valuation of stock 26
Ownership of books and records 111

Payroll fraud 25
Preparing and reporting information 74
Preparing financial statements 39
Prevention of Corruption Act 1906 30
Prevention of Corruption Act 1916 30
Proceeds of Crime Act 2002 36
Professional and technical competence 6

Professional behaviour 8
Professional liability 109
Professional negligence 109
Psychological contract 70, 83
Public Bodies Corrupt Practices Act 1889 30
Public interest 5
Public Interest Disclosure Act 1998 80

Questioning 48

Recommendations and referrals 90
Referral fee 91
Remuneration policy 98
Reports 51
Requesting help 48
Resolving conflict 48
Resolving ethical conflicts 17
Respect 67
Respect for confidentiality and privacy 76
Retention of documents 112

Safeguards 6, 16, 29, 105, 106
Second opinion 101
Self interest 71, 87
Self review 71, 87
Self-employed 18
Self-interest 105
Self-interest threats 15
Self-review 105
Self-review threats 15
Serious Organised Crime Agency (SOCA) 36
Stakeholders 28, 43, 64, 83
Supply of Goods and Services Act 1982 94

Taxation services 39
Teeming and lading 26
Terms 38
Terrorism Act 2000 36
Theft 25
Threats 15
Trust 67

Understating expenses 26

Verbal agreement 38

Whistle blowing 80
Working relationships and interactions 76
Written records 13